LOST VILI
of
TELFORD

George Evans

S.B. Publications

By the same author:
Wellington in Old Picture Postcards, European Library, 1987,
From Inkwell to I.B.M., The Story of Orleton Park School, 1990,
Wellington; A Portrait in Old Photographs and Picture Postcards, S.B. Publications, 1990.

Dedicated to Naomi and All Friends Round The Wrekin.

First published in 1991 by S.B. Publications,
Unit 2, Old Station Yard, Pipe Gate,
Market Drayton, Shropshire, TF9 4HY

© Copyright George Evans, 1991
Photographs and Text.

All rights reserved. No part of this publication may be reproduced, stored in a retrieval system, or transmitted in any form, or by an means, electronic or mechanical, photocopying, recording or otherwise, without the prior permission of the publisher.

ISBN 1 870708 78 4

Typeset, printed and bound by Manchester Free Press,
Paragon Mill, Jersey St., Manchester, M4 6FP. Tel: 061-236 8822

CONTENTS

Page
Preface 4
Introduction 5

LOST VILLAGES OF TELFORD

Page

1. Admaston 7
2. Apley 9
3. Aqueduct 11
4. Arleston 13
5. Benthall Edge 15
6. Blists Hill 17
7. Bratton 19
8. Brookside 21
9. Coalbrookdale 23
10. Coalport 25
11. Dawley 27
12. Dawley Bank 29
13. Donnington 31
14. Donnington Wood 33
15. Doseley 35
16. Dothill 37
17. Hadley 39
18. Halesfield 41
19. Hinkshay 43
20. Hollinswood 45
21. Horsehay 47
22. Horton 49
23. Hortonwood 51
24. Ironbridge 53
25. Jackfield 55
26. Ketley 57
27. Ketley Bank 59
28. Lawley 61
29. Lawley Common 63
30. Leegomery 65
31. Lightmoor 67
32. Little Dawley 69
33. Madeley 71

Page

34. Malinslee 73
35. Muxton 75
36. Nash 77
37. Nedge Hill 79
38. Newdale 81
39. Oakengates 83
40. Old Park 85
41. Orleton 87
42. Overdale 89
43. Priorslee 91
44. Randlay 93
45. Red Hill 95
46. Red Lake 97
47. St. Georges 99
48. Shawbirch 101
49. Snedshill 103
50. Spring Village 105
51. Stafford Park 107
52. Steeraway 109
53. Stirchley 111
54. Sutton Hill 113
55. Telford Centre 115
56. The Humbers 117
57. The Rock 119
58. Trench 121
59. Trench Lock 123
60. Tweedale 125
61. Watling Street 127
62. Wellington 129
63. Wombridge 131
64. Woodside 133
65. Wrockwardine 135
66. Wrockwardine Wood 137

Map of the Population of Telford in 1966
Map of Basic Geology
Telford in 1808 — Map by Robert Baugh
Map of Communities in this book
Communications
A Brief history of the area
Bibliography

Front cover: The Wrekin from Lawley Common; The Telford Statue, Telford Square.
Back cover: Geological wall, Queensway (A442).
Title page: M54 and The Wrekin from Red Lake.

PREFACE

The coming of Telford has made a great difference to this area and in the year that Telford Development Corporation finally winds down we thought we would celebrate with a book. Its title, 'Lost Villages of Telford', emphasises the importance of the many small communities which make up the fascinating mosaic of the landscape. We found no less than sixty-six different places, most of which can be called villages, though some are towns and others by no means lost.

Much of my information has come from the books and maps which are listed later, though there is also local knowledge of my own (I have lived in Wellington most of my 68 years and worked in Ketley, Hadley and Dawley) and from friends.

The photographs are my own, most taken this year (1991) with a Practica MTL3 and a Zeiss 50mm lens on Ilford FP4 film. Looking for the best scene with the right light has been a fascinating experience, making me take another look at familiar places. I have tried to show what I thought was interesting about each 'village', so many of them are of buildings which have survived from earlier times.

The maps shown were drawn by myself, except for the oldest, Robert Baugh's excellent county map of 1808, a copy of which I found in the Royal Geographical Society's map room.

The question whether Telford has been a mixed blessing or a mitigated disaster is like asking if the glass is half full or half empty. I have tried to describe places as they are and enough history to explain how they came to be. For most of us 'natives' there are positive and negative aspects to change and we try to make the best of what is there. The Development Corporation built the best new town they could, but I sometimes wish they had not built one at all.

The best of Telford is its people; not only the majority who were here before it came but many of the newcomers who are glad to be here now. We are far more cosmopolitan. There are still 'jockeys' who can 'talk broad', though not enough. The old accents are losing ground, though I did hear a young Sikh lad with a Hadley accent the other day.

What of the future? Will the rather arbitrary Telford boundary remain? Will it prosper? How will it change? We shall see.

In the meantime this is a book for anyone interested in the fascinating collection of communities I have called 'Lost Villages of Telford'. I can only hope it is as interesting to read as it was to write.

George Evans,
Wellington

The Gatehouse to Orleton Hall.

INTRODUCTION

Was this area all dereliction and obsolescence, pit mounds and slag heaps, general misery, before it became Telford? This has so often been implied that we should begin by looking at the facts, rather than the opinions of outsiders or official propaganda.

Before Telford half the land area was used for agriculture; one third was built up. Some of the remaining sixth was derelict, but it was regenerating naturally and much had an attractive scrubland which was by no means displeasing and provided pleasant walks almost everywhere.

But we should start at the very beginning. Most of the land is underlain by carboniferous rocks, rich in coal, iron ore and clay. These were the foundations for the very early industries which flourished in the 18th. century.

Overlying these rocks are clays, sands and gravels brought by glaciers in the last Ice Age. There is evidence of continuous occupation of the lands around The Wrekin from Neolithic times to the present day.

For much of this time it has been a large forest with gradually growing clearings for farming. Most of the place names here have the syllable 'ley' or 'lee' which imply a forest clearing. By the 17th. century there was a realisation that there were riches under the ground worth more than could be earned from farming. At first most of the mines were shallow but gradually they were deepened as more equipment and capital was available.

Dawley and later Telford were to relocate people from the West Midlands. Most of the houses and factories were built on green fields. The new infrastructure cut across the old road and rail systems and the initial intention was to create a unified, centralised town. But the rugged individuality of the local towns and villages made sure that their unique characters have survived; and some of the 'new' communities have developed on the same lines too.

This book is a celebration of sixty-six unique communities, many of which are nothing like as lost as they might seem.

Stafford Park.

Farmhouse in Bratton Road.

Headquarters of Salop Sand & Gravel.

1. ADMASTON

Admaston is much older than it looks. The name derives from Saxon and means 'Eadmund's Homestead'; the Domesday Book records it as being held by Almund, who was a free man, and his son Alward, from the Earl of Shrewsbury. It had a value of seven shillings for its two hides, having three and a half ploughs, four villagers and seven smallholders.

The often repeated statement that Telford was all dereliction and pit mounds is clearly a nonsense here. All the building has been on good agricultural land; modern gardens show its fertility.

In the mid-18th century the rural village grew into a small spa when the natural saline spring at Admaston Spa was developed. The geology was similar to Kingley Wych, near Preston, where a salt works once operated.

The spa building had a chequered career. It opened in 1750 and by 1805 there was an hotel, rebuilt in the 1840s round a courtyard. It had a colonnaded entrance, clock tower and a bath house. From the 1860s it declined, became a private house in 1890 but was an hotel again from 1928 to 1933. After this it was a chicken farm and a lodging house. The nearby sewage works (built in 1911) cannot have improved its prospects.

At its height Admaston Spa was much visited for its waters, advertised as so efficacious that even frail ladies were enabled to walk up The Wrekin. At one time it became a centre for Freemasons. During the Second World War it was the headquarters of Admaston Home Guard Platoon, who successfully defended the village from Nazi invasion. The main building has now been renovated and is the centre of an impressive development of neo-Georgian houses.

Interesting buildings include the timber framed Admaston Farm and Admaston Hall, a remarkable three storey, five bay house with a 'semi-detached' farm at the rear. There is also The Oaklands, an extremely attractive Victorian house now owned by Salop Sand and Gravel.

Two railway lines passed through Admaston. The Halt, on the Wellington-Shrewsbury line opened in 1851 but closed in 1964. The office and signal box were within an arch of the road bridge. This halt was in part responsible for the growth in population between those dates. The Wellington-Market Drayton line closed in 1967 and is now a footpath — part of the Silkin Way.

The only public house in Admaston itself is the Pheasant, a pleasant brick building on the main east-west road which is thought to be part of the Portway, a very ancient route. Admaston House, on the Wellington Road, was for some time the home of R.D. Newill, solicitor and clerk to Wellington magistrates. It is now a community centre. Recent developments have expanded Admaston's role as a middle-class residential suburb at the expense of farmland. Once it was described as the wealthiest village in Shropshire and the large houses recently built, particularly to the east near the spa suggest that this may still be the case.

Admaston Spa & Clock House.

Remains of Old Apley Castle.

The Princess Royal Hospital.

2. APLEY

The name Apley seems to be Saxon and to imply a forest clearing devoted to apples — presumably an orchard. John de Praeres of Dothill owned it in 1282 but by 1317 it belonged to Sir Alan of Charlton and remained in his family until Walter James Charlton sold it to TDC in 1971. Some of the Charlton family were called Meyrick or Charlton-Meyrick.

There was a licence to crenelate (fortify) in 1327, probably on or near the site of a previous house. This house, enlarged in 17th century and then badly damaged in the Civil War, remains. The Civil War, later neglect and a disastrous attempt to repair it in TDC times have all caused great damage; there is much local debate as to which caused the greatest vandalism.

A new house was built in the late 18th century and enlarged in the mid 19th century. The final result was a huge building, late Georgian to the north and ornamental Victorian in the south. It reflected the value of royalties on coal and iron earned by ownership of land on the coalfield. Ornamental gardens and woods were laid out by St. John Chiverton Charlton. There is a story that one of the Charlton-Meyrick family was drowned in the Apley pool and that in consequence the windows in the north part of the house, which overlooks the pool were kept closed and shuttered.

This final house was demolished in 1955 and there is little trace of it. The site is now a group of birch trees though some foundations have been excavated. The gardens were so full of wild life that the Shropshire Wildlife Trust designated them as a prime site for nature conservation but after several years of being 'tidied up' by TDC so much of the natural vegetation has been destroyed and so many of the birds and animals have gone away that this designation has had to be cancelled.

Maxell factory.

The Aqueduct.

Chapel, now Scout Headquarters.

3. AQUEDUCT

For once this old settlement has no pretensions to have been in the Domesday book as the aqueduct giving it its name was built to carry a spur of the Shropshire Union Canal which opened in 1792. However, the importance of the canal is shown by the fact that it carried, in tub boats, much of the coal that fired the Coalbrookdale furnaces. The grey limestone of the aqueduct is now well worn, but still there to be seen.

After the decline of water transport the canal bed was transformed into a railway, though it was necessary to straighten it out and a few bends of the old canal are still visible. These are used as fishing pools. The railway now has gone too and the route is a footpath, part of Silkin Way.

The local road pattern has been much altered since the new town and Aqueduct Road, once part of the A442 Bridgnorth-Wellington route has been cut by Queensway and is impassable. There is a fine pub and Tunnel Cottages, but otherwise it is impossible to find the settlement which used to be pronounced 'Ackyduck'.

The place is now a collection of new houses, many of which are quite attractive, with a primary school and shopping centre. The industrial past is gone and mainly forgotten; the present settlement has almost no connection with what has gone before. Many of the present inhabitants cannot direct a stranger to the aqueduct which gave the place its name — that includes two postmen I asked.

Silkin Way.

Britannia Inn.

Arleston Manor

Shops and flats, Dawley Road.

4. ARLESTON

Nowadays it is difficult to distinguish between the village of Arleston and the Wellington estate of that name. To make things more difficult there is now a boundary between the parishes of Wellington and Ketley which puts the remains of the old village in Ketley but leaves most of the newer houses in Wellington.

What is usually meant by 'Arleston' now consists of three large estates built by Wellington Urban District Council, beginning just before the second world war and finished in the 1960s, together with more recent Manor Rise and the old Arleston Village. The UDC built well and many of the houses are now owner occupied. The estates were built in an east-west sequence, 'A site' being east of Arleston Lane, 'B site' between Dawley Road and Arleston Lane and 'C site' west of Dawley Road. The latter estate includes Barn Farm and Ercall Junior schools. Most of this land was originally in the township of Watling Street or in Wellington Hay, the main deer enclosure of the Royal Forest of The Wrekin rather than Arleston. For a time The Wrekin Forest was called the forest of Mount Gilbert and the road south of Barn Farm School recalls that name.

Tucked away between the old village and the M54 is Arleston Manor, at one time called Arleston House, a very fine timber framed house (see photograph), said to have been built as a Royal hunting lodge. The house was restored in the early 20th century and again in 1979. One gable is dated 1614, the other 1640 though the plan is late 16th century and there is evidence of 16th century work inside. It is currently being developed as an hotel.

The village, as a site, is much older; the name has been suggested as deriving from 'Eardwulf's tun', indicating Saxon origins. It was thought to have been one of Wellington's berewicks in 1066 and a substantial part of it belonged to Wellington manor. Lord Forester became the main owner but the 5th baron sold the estate in 1918.

Between Arleston Lane and the dual carriageway A518 is a development called Wellington Park — presumably as a tribute to Wellington Town Council which most strongly opposed planning permission, supporting Wrekin District Council, Telford Development Corporation and Shropshire County Council but losing at a planning inquiry! This is a somewhat upmarket version of an American shopping mall, strategically placed near the M54 junction but also Glynwed's iron works.

Tesco superstore, 'Wellington Park'.

Old water mill.

Bridge over disused Severn Valley Railway.

5. BENTHALL EDGE

Very little of Benthall Edge is within Telford's boundary; there is just a strip alongside the River Severn opposite the Wharfage at Ironbridge. The Edge itself is a river cliff, now mainly wooded, and having a nature trail. Its height is often exaggerated in old prints as an impressive background to the iron bridge.

Alongside Bridge Bank, in a steep dingle, is a stream which used to have a most impressive watermill with a huge wheel, as large as the famous Laxey wheel in the Isle of Man, and of a similar design. It worked on the 'under-overshot' principle — that is the water was carried high in a trough but discharged before the wheel, turning it towards the source.

There are a few old houses and the toll house for the bridge. A large brick viaduct built partly into the hill used to carry the Severn Valley Railway towards Buildwas, with a junction for Much Wenlock. There is still a railway which crosses the Albert Edward bridge, though this only carries fuel to the power station.

The railway station by the iron bridge is now a car park. Between here and Jackfield is Ladywood, leading to the free bridge, an historic pre-stressed concrete structure surmounted by a bailey bridge. Agreement for a replacement has been difficult to obtain in the late 1980s and early 1990s.

Composed mainly of Wenlock limestone, there are many quarries and mines on Benthall Edge, all of which are now disused. The limestone was carried across the river for use as a flux in the many furnaces of Ironbridge and Madeley Wood. The nature trail is constructed on the steep cliff and passes many interesting lime loving plants.

Benthall Edge viaduct, River Severn and power station.

Coalport Road.

Preserved engines.

6. BLISTS HILL
(BLESSES or BLISSERS HILL)

Off Coalport Road, formerly known as Dabbelly Lane, is the main section of the Ironbridge Gorge Museum. It is one of the most important museums of the world, a World Heritage Site, yet it is only of recent origin. Only forty years ago Michael Rix, the inventor of the expression 'industrial archaeology' was trying to interest the general public in the east Shropshire area and the beginnings of what is now called the Industrial Revolution. Whether the museum accurately depicts the atmosphere of the 18th and 19th century industry here is debatable but it certainly attracts the public. Although there was a considerable industrial complex here many of the exhibits are imported from other sites and all have been somewhat sanitised and romanticised. If a true picture was shown the museum would be empty.

In many ways the site is ideal. Blists Hill furnaces closed in 1912. There was a derelict canal, part of which it was possible to reclaim using volunteer labour. There had been clay, brick and sanitary pipe industries, coal and ironstone mines and manufacturers, a disused railway, woodland on pit and slag mounds; in fact many of the features of 18th century industrial development. It was easily accessed by road and it was very derelict and available. Historical buildings in the new town were going to be demolished and should be preserved. Telford Development Corporation had money and needed an historical scenario. All these factors contributed to the museum.

Like Madeley Wood, Coalport, and The Lloyds the small settlement which had developed around the many factories, mines and quarries stagnated in the 19th and early 20th centuries. In fact there is almost nothing on the first edition Ordnance Survey map of around 1841. Apart from Great Hay and its farmhouse there were only little cottages on the future museum site and these were mostly derelict. The street of buildings now on exhibition have almost all been brought in and erected in their new position. There are perhaps more old buildings on this site than there ever were in the days depicted by the museum.

So Blists Hill is indeed a lost village — lost and re-created. Or perhaps recreated, for its function lies in recreation as well as information. It is still well worth a long visit.

General view of the museum.

Bratton Farm.

Wheatfield outside Telford boundary.

7. BRATTON

Although Bratton is marked as part of Telford on the street map, most of the ancient township is to the north-east of the boundary. What is now marked as Bratton was until recently part of Admaston.

Bratton hamlet is part of the Weald Moors, an area of marsh and shallow lakes left by the last Ice Age and the subject of drainage schemes ever since. At domesday it was said to have land for four ploughs but the five smallholders had nothing and it was almost waste. They probably lived well enough on fish and wildfowl but would not have told the officials.

There are building sites and fine new houses in what is now termed Bratton, the part of Telford, though most of Bratton proper remains in farming. The housing extends into Admaston and Shawbirch, which is being developed as a village centre.

Bratton's most important building is the Gate Inn, with its famous sign;

This gate hangs well
And hinders none,
Refresh and pay
And carry on.

This is written on a gate hanging high above the entrance. Across the road is the start of Silkin Way footpath on the abandoned Wellington to Crewe railway. Silkin was claimed to be the 'father of new towns' — so presumably was responsible for Ur of the Chaldes and Viroconium Cornoviorum!

The Gate Inn sign.

Community Centre Mural.

8. BROOKSIDE

There is little historical to say about Brookside. It is a large Development Corporation housing estate, designed on a modified version of the Radcliffe plan in the 1970s. The balloon-shaped Brookside Avenue surrounds the estate, restricting and confining it. Narrow roads enter from this perimeter road without joining each other and some have a connection to the shopping centre, pastoral centre, community centre, probation office and two schools.

To a visitor it may appear claustrophobic and introverted. It has been designed and built to a theory which included the separation of vehicles and pedestrians. Certainly it is a short walk from any house to school or shops and the provision of communal rooms has been relatively generous. This was intended to foster a sense of neighbourhood. Footpaths are well made and encourage walking. Many trees have been planted which give a feeling of being in a wood full of houses.

Most of the houses and flats are of similar design, though there is a wide variety of sizes. Intended to be rented, some have been bought since the 'right to buy' laws and it is interesting to see the individual 'customisation' of owner-occupied dwellings. A major problem is the apparently haphazard distribution of house numbers, which visitors find confusing.

Brookside's history is all to come. It is for the inhabitants to decide if the theory of the Radburn Principle works out for them in practice. No one else is qualified.

Estate scene.

Coalbrookdale Works.

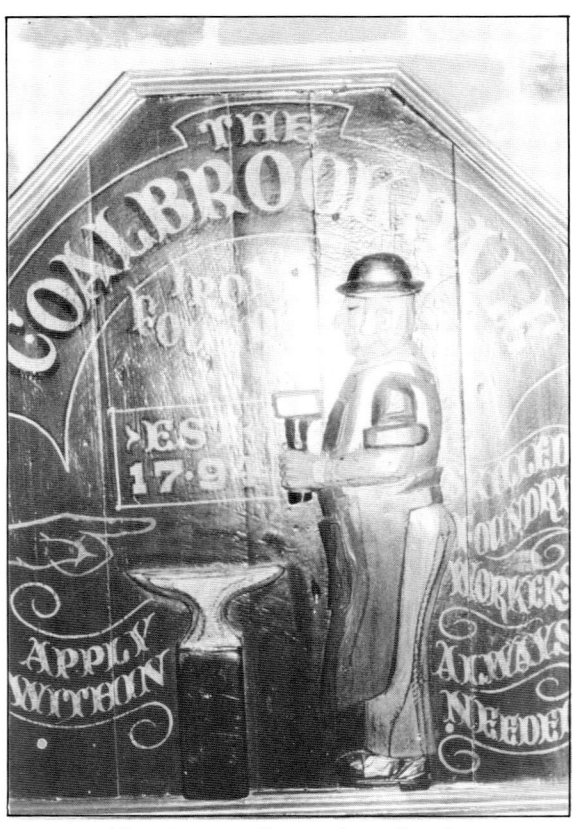
Advertisement for workers found at the Cuckoo Oak.

9. COALBROOKDALE

Was there ever such a descriptive name? Yet its origin is the valley of the Caldebrook, which was operating a mill in the early 16th century. Although giving its name to the coalfield the rocks in 'The Dale' as it is often called locally are not productive measures, being Silurian limestone and Wenlock shales. All the eastern part of Madeley is middle and lower coal measures; with both coal and iron easily available. The raw materials for the iron industry are nearby but not actually — apart from limestone — in Coalbrookdale.

Before Abraham Darby brought fame to the area with his coke furnace there was an iron industry well established, using the usual fuel, charcoal. In fact his first furnace was previously used in this way by Sir Basil Brooke and is dated 1638. Darby's first date as all children should know is 1709. The stream was extensively used to power the blowing mechanisms necessary for the blast furnaces and hammers in forges. Six pools were made by damming the stream to provide reservoirs of energy.

Holy Trinity Church.

Old Coalport china works.

The Free Bridge.

10. COALPORT

Mention of Coalport around The Wrekin brings the instant response — china. This is still held in high regard locally, though 'proper Coalport' excludes porcelain made since the firm moved to Staffordshire in 1926 in spite of the excellent display of fine new china at the old works. In many local homes there are treasured collections of china, usually family heirlooms, from this works, started by John Rose and continuing for 130 years. Most are now augmented by modern work.

Coalport was a 'new town', planned and founded in 1792, when the Shropshire Canal was extended here. It was intended to become a chief port on the River Severn, connecting with the canal by the inclined plane and dealing with most of the goods produced on the Coalbrookdale coalfield and the necessary imports. This, however, was not to be, and although there was success it was not on such a scale.

The Tar Tunnel is a strange story. It was constructed to provide access to a mine, which it never actually reached. Whilst it was being built bitumen began to seep through the bricks and soon there was a barrel a day of this rich bounty. Gradually the seepage diminished but not before it had earned a fortune for its owners. A small chemical industry grew up nearby.

The present view of Coalport is mainly of exhibits from a 'glorious past', though there is fortunately no reconstruction of the smell of burnt bones which were added to make the bone china. The inclined plane and the sections of canal top and bottom are well displayed, as is the Tar Tunnel, and the China Museum deserves its international fame.

Coalport iron bridge from Woodbridge.

High Street with Captain Webb Memorial.

The Old Market Place.

11. DAWLEY

The Dawley Book, produced by Great Dawley Parish Council, describes Dawley as 'A small town in the middle of the old Shropshire coalfield', which is a good beginning. At first it was an Anglo-Saxon village in The Wrekin forest, one of the parts of the manor of Wellington. The forest was gradually cleared, but the agricultural character changed as the coal, iron and clay under the ground became more important than the earth above. All that remains of the ancient village is the 12th century font at Holy Trinity Church. Dawley Castle, which was destroyed in the Civil War, became a stone quarry and its remains are buried under a pit mound south of the church.

The mineral deposits were close to the surface, especially west of the Lightmoor fault, which crosses the parish from north to south. At first mining was simple and inexpensive and 'everyone who had a bucket had a pit'. The result was a great number of 'back garden' mines. often bell-pits. Later, when it was necessary to mine deeper, pumping engines and winding gear were needed so large companies with capital became involved. The Coalbrookdale Company was the largest, but there were others, some of which engaged charter masters to organise the work.

The raw materials mined were used in local factories — foundries, steelworks and brickworks, some being sent out by canal and later by train, as several lines went through and near the town. During the 19th century some of these industries declined as the Black Country prospered, and many local people moved with the jobs — which probably explains why the expression 'going all round The Wrekin' is so common there. In recent years there has been a return from the West Midlands to Dawley.

Before becoming a New Town, Dawley had an excellent shopping centre with a Saturday market in the Market Hall. It was almost all in one street, but served the town well. The unusually ornate Methodist Church gave High Street distinction. Many of the mounds were recolonising and gradually returning to forest. All was certainly not the 'gloom and doom' claimed by the developers. Schools, including the Phoenix, Pool Hill and the old National (where I taught in the early 1950s), were generally good. Now much is changed, and it is for the people of Dawley to decide if it is not for the better.

Dawley's greatest asset is its people, with their individual accent and sense of humour, from which stems many local expressions. The two most famous are Matthew Webb, who first swam the Channel and Edith Pargeter (Ellis Peters,) whose books, especially of Brother Cadfael, deserve their popularity. It is also a town of many clubs; a neighbourly place, expert at raising money for good causes.

High Street.

Baptist Church.

Evangelical Church.

12. DAWLEY BANK

Occupying high ground to the north of Great Dawley, Dawley Bank was a straggling industrial settlement which is now in-filled with a great variety of modern houses, some planned in groups and some apparently haphazard infilling. The result is a fascinating mixture of ages and styles of buildings. The largest remnants of the past are the church and the Baptist chapel; Ladygrove School is the biggest modern building.

The original road pattern, which had developed naturally to accommodate the needs of local people has been chopped up and new roads planned to favour fast drivers have been imposed. An example is Old Office Road, which should go on to Park Road but is cut through several times so as not to impede new roads such as Concorde and Dawley Green Way. However it is possible to walk the route if you don't mind sprinting across Concorde.

In the early 19th century what had been an agricultural area with some shallow pits developed much mining and industry and the population rapidly expanded. By the latter part of the same century things were in such a decline that there was an emigration officer in Dawley Bank and many families went off to Australia. Many more departed for the Black Country and other industrial areas where their skills earned them work not available here.

The chief occupation at the height of Dawley Bank's popularity was mining. The Lightmoor Fault is between Dawley Bank and Malinslee, and the land to the west of it has shallow coal seams that were easy to work without expensive equipment. Nearly all the area has been mined for coal, iron or clay — in some places for all three — in small back-yard pits. By 1965 most of the land between Heath Hill and Old Park was covered in debris from pits or furnaces. There were also a great many shafts, most of which had to be made safe.

In many ways Dawley Bank could be said to be a microcosm of the development of Telford. First there was agriculture, then a surge of mining, industry and population, followed by a great decline and finally clearance with redevelopment, resulting in an interesting mix of old and new. With its raised position Dawley Bank has very fine views of The Wrekin, especially from its newest pub, the Wrekin View.

The Bull's Head.

Our Lady of the Rosary Catholic Church.

Shops from Winifred's Drive.

13. DONNINGTON

Nearly all of what is now called Donnington was built in the late 1930s and early 1940s. With the Second World War imminent the government of the day decided to move the great army supply depot away from the vulnerable London area to Shropshire. The result was the Central Ordnance Depot and the associated housing at Donnington. There are still many people in the area who have London accents, which were distinctive before the whole of east Shropshire became cosmopolitan. In many ways the depot dominates Donnington, providing employment for most of the inhabitants, though not to the extent that it did in the beginning when it was almost the only employer.

The depot itself consists mainly of huge sheds covering many acres. Some are administrative, other stores. An island on the A518 surmounted by three artillery guns marks one of the entrances. The COD is surrounded by a wire fence and has security guards. In spite of this there have been unexplained fires costing hundreds of millons of pounds. Within the perimeter is some housing for forces personnel and their families. The old Wellington to Stafford railway line used to pass through but now ends at sidings within the depot. There is a rather odd looking loop of the Telford boundary north of Donnington which encloses military accommodation.

Employment in Donnington has been more stable since the depot arrived than most nearby places, due to the miliary's need to keep key personnel. Jobs are stable but the amount of work needed fluctuates according to the reqirements for and of the forces. There are still some 'displaced persons' as they were called; Serbs, Croats, Poles and others who arrived during the second world war and did not return home for various reasons. Later these people were called European Voluntary Workers and many supplemented the depot's labour force. To begin with the Londoners felt displaced too and formed their own churches, clubs and societies. Donnington was not like the city and the natives referred to the depot as 'The Dump.'

Donnington has been less affected by the new town than most parts of Telford, as it was fully built up and had no room for further development. It was already a new town.

Guns on Garrison Roundabout.

Sculpture in Granville Country Park.

14. DONNINGTON WOOD

Like Wrockwardine, Donnington had a remnant of The Wrekin Forest which was allocated to the village. It was gradually cleared for agriculture and found to have useful deposits of coal, iron and clay. These were probably first used by Wombridge Priory, but their greatest development was by the Chartons of Apley and the Leveson-Gower family. The latter were the principal landowners and owned the Lilleshall Company. A canal was also built. The biggest coal mine, also the largest in East Shropshire, was the Granville, named after Granville Leveson-Gower.

The Granville pit was taken over by the National Coal Board and was Shropshire's last deep mine. It was over a thousand feet deep and had modern equipment. Local teachers, including myself, used to take parties of children down to the coal face. The seams are much faulted and there was often talk of closure; the mine extended far underground. There is a retainer wall of Queensway (A442) at St. Georges which depicts the faulted seams. Gas was a problem until it was piped to Wellington gas works for domestic use. Water, which also had to be extracted, was used to balance the canals.

The Granville colliery, then employing 560 men, was closed in 1979. Since then the site has been reclaimed; some of the colliery buildings preserved and a large area has become the Granville Country Park. This is now a Local Nature Reserve and contains not only interesting species but also a unique ecology which has developed on the recolonised industrial sites. It is hoped that this will continue to be appreciated and preserved; there is always a danger that, like similar sites, the flora will be municipalised and tidied up.

In 1991 there was almost no housing in Donnington Wood but there are plans for large scale re-development. The past has been largely erased; the future looks interesting.

Old colliery buildings off Muxton Lane.

Railway Bridge.

St. Luke's Church.
(now a private house)

15. DOSELEY

Most of Doseley is an industrial area between Little Dawley and Horsehay, Spring Village and Lightmoor. In 1928 the Doseley Brick Company, (later the Doseley Pipe Company), one of the Johnston group of companies, made common bricks from the overburden of the basalt quarries there. The works changed to making salt-glazed pipes in 1932 which continues.

The quarry extracted black basalt, similar to the 'dhu stone' on Clee Hill. It is columnar in structure and has been in its time a tourist attraction. There is said to be a mineral spring within the quarry area which is still sometimes used. The stone was used as an aggregate for concrete and pipes were made, though when quarrying ceased in 1961, due to the exhaustion of the reserves, the factory used rock from Leaton quarries for this purpose.

Doseley began as a wood clearing and the name Pawn Hatchett, near Doseley probably refers to a gate leading into a wood in medieval times. Woods were then valuable assets, providing all the various timber products for everyday use as well as house building. They were also fuel stores and often pasture for pigs and poultry.

St. Luke's church was built in 1844, designed by R. Griffiths of Broseley, to provide for the new parish of Little Dawley, but on the amalgamation of churches in Central Telford in 1980 it was declared redundant and sold and is now a house.

There is some housing along Frame Lane (which according to old maps seems to pre-date the name Doseley) and St. Lukes Road, but otherwise Doseley is largely an industrial estate from which a variety of firms operate.

Johnston Pipes.

Dothill Lake with fishermen.

Hawkstone and Haughmond Courts.

16. DOTHILL

Assumed to be one of Wellington's berewicks or outlying places at domesday, Dothill was never a big settlement until the last few years. It was incorporated into Wellington manor and cost the first known tenant, John de Preares 1/6 of a knight's service to Giles of Erdington, Lord of Wellington. Other occupiers included the Horton family, some of whom were tax collectors, and the Stephensons. The Barons Forester owned the house and much of the manor for a long time but by 1922 the chief landowner was Ernest Groom, the Wellington timber merchant.

In 1952 it belonged to Harry Hodgson, the Canadian managing director of Joseph Sankey's Hadley Castle works. He sold most of Dothill to Wellington Urban District Council. Subsequently the southern part of the area was developed for housing, including two tall blocks of flats, originally called Hawkestone Court and Haughmond Court. The northern part was not developed in the 1950s and 1960s because it was below the level of the sewage works. Recent proposals to complete the development caused a furore; a modified version of the plans is now being built and there is planned provision for a nature conservation area. The preservation of a wetland habitat may have been made difficult by the draining of the area.

The moated house, which was at one time quite extensive, has now gone, and apart from some foundations there are few signs of either the manor house or its farm. What does remain, however, is a small section of moat and two large lakes, one called Dothill Pool, the other the Tee Lake. There is little trace either of the extensive gardens apart from an obviously artificial mound. There are stories of jousting from boats in the lake and crowds of spectators.

The most southerly part of Dothill, on Spring Hill, was for many years used for the annual wool sales. From here towards the north has gradually been developed for housing, until it is now almost all built over as far as Shawbirch.

Major housing developments are taking place as I write, though not with the agreement of many of the inhabitants of the earlier houses in the southern part, who had long cherished the open spaces. Some conservation of trees, wetlands and hedges has been promised. It remains to be seen if this will really happen.

Dothill County School.

Chassis Sculpture.

Manor Heights & Footbridge.

17. HADLEY

'Holding of Reginald the Sheriff (under Earl Roger),' says the Domesday Book, 'Geoffrey holds it from him. Wihtric and Alric held it as two manors. In lordship 1 plough; 2 slaves; 8 smallholders with ½ plough; a further 2½ ploughs would be possible there. A mill at 2s; woodland, 1 league. Value before 1066, 37s now 15s; he found it waste'.

The terse prose of the Domesday Book tells of another time, yet it is the same place, Hadley. Older than, say, Newport, though it would be difficult to guess looking at modern Hadley. Who could imagine that the old village was once rented for a sparrowhawk and had three miles of forest?

What of Hadley nowadays? We all think of Sankey's, Haybridge Steel, The Bush, Manor School, the Methodist and Holy Trinity Churches, the Sikh Temple, the Male Voice Choir, Manor Heights and the overpass. The large new estates in Leegomery are part of another story.

Hadley Castle Works has been a large employer for many years, though it no longer has 6,265 on the payroll as in 1978. When the author worked there briefly in 1941 the factory was producing spitfire parts, mines, bombs, and bailey bridges as well as the inevitable wheels.

Before Sankey's were puddling furnaces, owned by Nettlefolds (the N in GKN). John Bailey, I am told, drove a mule train with panniers laden with bricks to build furnaces, the arches of which were uncovered when press pits were excavated. There may be a connection with Thomas Guest (the G in GKN) of Broseley, who set up an iron works in South Wales. Here were built tramcars and railway waggons for Japan before Sankey of Bilston expanded to motor car panels and wheels, with raw materials coming in and products going out on the Shropshire Union Canal.

Joseph Sankey was an orphan boy who 'served his time' making blank trays and became a craftsman and later an engineer and manager. The firm he set up in Hadley came to employ large numbers of men and women for many miles around. The Haybridge steel company, now no more, used to make steel wire; watching the snakes of glowing steel darting about on the shopfloor was a fascinating sight.

Culturally Hadley is far richer than it looks; there is an excellent choir and a long tradition of good singing. The Women's Institute's Jerusalem is the best for miles. Indian and West Indian immigrants have brought their own songs and dances, though there is much integration. It was interesting to hear a young black friend from Manor Heights, (a tower block) walking over the 'Hadley Pier' (the overpass) say he was 'going down the village'.

Haybridge Hall.

Kemberton Road.

Coppice Farm Roundabout.

18. HALESFIELD

The Development Corporation's largest industrial estate can hardly be described as a lost village; there was never a village to be lost and there certainly is not one there now. However, it is a part of Telford, and therefore it was decided to describe the area.

Begun in 1967, the estate was intended to provide space for the various industries which the Corporation hoped it would attract to Dawley and later on Telford. The whole area was acquired by the Corporation and firms were either to build their own premises or factories would be built for them to rent or buy. Most of the building was done by TDC — utility steel framed sheds presumably built to be easily re-arranged or demolished. Some are struggling with lack of amenities, others are smart, surrounded by lawns and trees.

Before the building of Halesfield the land was open fields sloping gently down to the Mad Brook which flowed through the centre. The brook has been culverted. On the first edition of the Ordnance Survey one inch map, published in 1841, there were very few houses between the Cuckoo Oak inn and Brockton Hall. Equally there were no pits, mounds or works. It was a 'green field' site.

The estate is laid out in a grid pattern, though not slavishly. The main roads are Kemberton Road (A4169) from east to west and the north-south spine called Haldane. A large number of firms of various nationalities have now set up here. In general there has been much success, especially in plastics manufacture, though the list of manufactures is very diverse and quite fascinating.

Haldane looking south.

Three Crowns Inn.

The Mad Hatter's Tea Party.

19. HINKSHAY

A great deal of Hinkshay is now part of the Town Park, consisting of woodlands, playing fields and the field studies area created from old pools, mounds and wetlands by John Cotterill when he was an engineer and surveyor for Dawley UDC.

Like most of the Dawley area, Hinkshay was an industrial village in the early 19th century, having the Hinkshay ironworks. There was a light railway from the canal through Malinslee to the Old Park Ironworks. Eleven pits were opened between Hinkshay and Malinslee in the 1820s. But prosperity was short lived. The village suffered from the depression in the late 19th century and there was much poverty and consequent depopulation.

All that remains of the old days of prosperity is an excellent pub and the school, now a 'special school'. There are also a few of the old cottages, many of which used to have separate brew houses and pig styes, producing home cured bacon and home brewed ale. The Ever Ready factory has been making dry cell batteries since 1956 and in 1980 employed 2,000 people. It is on the end of a lane, surrounded by the Town Park but is too important a provider of employment to be moved away. There is little, fortunately to recall the 'bad old days'.

Although most of the Town Park is open space and woodland there is a substantial portion given up to entertaining children. Part of this is Wonderland, with its Snow White's cottage, Mad Hatter's Tea Party, Wrekin Giant and other features. Wonderland is well worth a visit, even without children.

Several recent small housing estates have been developed on reclaimed land, the most recent incomplete in 1991. As a village Hinkshay has prospered, suffered, declined, stagnated and is now mainly open space and modern houses. To judge from the atmosphere in the Three Crowns it is a good place to live.

Snow White's Cottage.

Play area at Downmead.

The Woodcutter.

20. HOLLINSWOOD

Holly Wood, from which Hollinswood gets its name, was once between Priorslee and Wombridge parishes. Would the present inhabitants prefer it to be called Hollywood? It has the rectory for the newly created parish of Central Telford, with a meeting room. Mass is also said in the community centre for Roman Catholics. In the mid 19th century there was a Hollinswood Iron Works, but it is not well documented and appears to have become the Eagle Iron Works. By the 1950s most of the area was derelict.

The modern housing estate is most conveniently placed; to the east, across Queensway (A442), is Stafford Park industrial estate, Telford shopping mall and the associated complex is just north and the Town Park is to the south. One could work, shop, play and go to school within a few minutes walk. There are also the Racquet Centre, Skating Rink, Cinema, night club etc., and it is still on the edge of open woodland. In addition there is a local shopping centre, community centre, two schools and a surgery. All the advantages of a large town are provided without the cramped, overcrowded feeling most towns have.

There were houses in Hollinswood before Telford, at least one factory, mines, railway and a canal; of these there is no trace now. It was probably not a true village which has been lost, rather a hamlet. Now there is a large modern village, planned as well as it could be, given the constraints of finance. Perhaps it is a model village.

The Community Centre.

Pool View, restored cottages.

Horsehay Pool.

21. HORSEHAY

There have been several phases to the history of Horsehay; forest, agriculture, iron founding, clay, basalt, forging, bridge building, cranes and residential with light industry. This was a very early site for the Coalbrookdale Company to develop; from the 1750s there was iron working using the new coke methods. Limestone was brought from Limekiln Woods, coal and iron ore (mined nearby), all in small tub waggons on the 'ginny rails' pulled by horses. The foundry was soon joined by a forge. Pools were made to provide for water power for the blast furnaces; the largest remains at Horsehay Pool. Simpson's Pool is in a disused basalt quarry, hidden in a wood.

When the iron industry declined there were bridges, roofs and girders; steel structures not only for local use but also for far afield — over the Zambezi for instance. Long loaders used to disrupt traffic taking bridge parts from Horsehay to ports for shipment.

There was brickmaking, basalt and slag for roads, pottery and the manufacture of lead figurines as well as engineering. Bridges were followed by heavy cranes — requiring much the same skills. Both the engineering entrepises were on the same site as the original foundry. This is now mainly cleared.

One of the pottery kilns was converted into a house called the roundhouse. An inn is called the All Labour in Vain, its sign depicting some people trying to wash the colour off a black boy. At one time it was thought offensive until it was realised the joke was on the natives, so it remains. There is a very active steam locomotive preservation trust, which has a short track and some rolling stock. This is most appropriate for the Sentinel steam waggons were developed here before moving to Shrewsbury.

A bypass will be opened in 1992 relieving traffic on the Wellington Road (A5223). Horsehay has many industrial achievements to boast but is now relatively quiet.

All Labour In Vain.

The Queen's Head.

22. HORTON

Horton is on the edge of the Weald Moors and the soil to the north has lake clay and alluvium. These moors are a remnant of the wetlands caused by the disruption of drainage after the last Ice Age. There were shallow lakes, bog, alder carr and marsh which over many centuries were drained. Before drainage they were wildfowling and fishing places, but gradually they became farmlands; excellent arable land where the drainage was most successful.

There was a manor at domesday, held by Erniet, under Warin, Pantulf and Earl Roger. In later times parts of Horton belonged to Lilleshall Abbey, the Morris-Eyton family and the Preston Hospital Trust. Not far to the west is an old brickworks and there was once the salt manufactory of Kinley Wych. The 1871 gazetteer records six farmers (two were women), one of whom was also a maltster, a blacksmith, a carpenter and an innkeeper (Horseshoe Inn).

Horton is now mainly a collection of brick cottages, many detached, along the road from Leegomery to The Humbers and Horton Lane. There is also the excellent Queen's Head inn. But it is within the new town boundary and is scheduled for industrial development so presumably it will become a part of the Hortonwood industrial estate.

There is now (1991) drainage work going on and various other preparations and site works. It looks as if it will not be long before Horton is lost forever in urban sprawl. Perhaps there will be claims and this too was all pit mounds and slag heaps before Telford.

Farm, Horton Lane.

Looking East.

23. HORTONWOOD

In 1086 Horton's Wood (Hortonwood) was waste; by the 17th century there were 15 cottagers and smallholders, but the population had risen to 266 by 1841 and was 352 in 1891. Most of these people, however, lived on the Trench Road, which would now not be thought of as Hortonwood but Trench.

The 1841 Ordnance Survey map shows Hortonwood to be all farmland with the exception of a row of houses (some of which are farms or small holdings) along the Wellington — Newport road, now called Trench Road. Small streams drain the land to the north, under the Shrewsbury Canal and into the Commission Drain. Eventually the water joined the Strine, and the Tern and flowed to the Bristol Channel via the River Severn.

The main A518 road has been remade to the north of the remnants of the Wellington — Stafford railway, and is now carrying most of the through traffic, leaving the old road to deal with local vehicles. This new road joins the re-aligned A442 at a very large island, the Trench Lock Interchange, between Hadley Castle works and the Central Ordnance Depot. There are new roads within Hortonwood Industrial Estate, providing the basic transport infrastucture for its development.

The former farmlands are now completely gone and in their place are prefabricated steel, concrete and glass factory buildings, many of which look rather temporary. Hortonwood's largest factory now is Epson; there are also Bischof and Klein, Omron and several others. Many of the factories are foreign owned and a large variety of plastics is among the items manufactured.

What village there has been at Hortonwood is still there; not lost but now called Trench. Otherwise there are factories where there used to be farms.

'Duke of Sutherland' Houses.

Bedlam Furnace.

Across the bridge from the Toll House.

24. IRONBRIDGE

There are sometimes references to 'the historic part of Telford' which assume that only Ironbridge has any history. The opposite could be argued, as Ironbridge cannot be older than 1779, the bridge's date, whereas Dawley, Hadley, Madeley and Wellington are very much older. However, there is no doubt about the fame of Ironbridge or that it is a most interesting place. So much has been written about the industrial archaeology of the gorge recently that is it easy to forget that only in the 1960s it was difficult to persuade most people that the early industrial remains were worth looking at or considering as part of local, national and world history.

Now it must be the best known place in Shropshire. Until the 19th century it was part of Madeley which was in the Borough of Much Wenlock. The 1871 Directory calls it a market town situated in a steep acclivity. The buildings are interesting if only as a wonder that they do not slide on their clay foundations into the gorge. Geologists like Andrew Jenkinson point out that the roads have been built on outcrops, avoiding the clay. There are often landslides and slumping on both sides of the river as the gorge is geologically new and far from stable. The bending of the bridge can be seen by comparing old photographs with modern ones, especially looking from the tollhouse towards the Tontine Hotel.

The wharfage, now often full of tourists, was once a thriving river port; the largest warehouse is a museum and others are restaurants and houses. There are traces of many foundries but only at Bedlam has there been a serious attempt to preserve and display one. The shops and market which once served the thriving little town are now busy with tourists, providing antiques and souvenirs, ice cream and snacks.

Between Ironbridge's high point as an industrial town and port and the present bustle of the tourist trade was a period of decline when there was little work and it was very run down. There was much criticism by local people of the money spent on restoration. They claimed that although it improved the town it did not help the inhabitants, most of whom could not afford the prices of restored houses and had to move out. There was also a loss of some facilities.

Ironbridge is not so much lost as completely changed. Trade no longer comes by barge or train but by car and coach. It is advertised as 'a good day out for the family' and many of its former inhabitants say its atmosphere is more like Blackpool than Ironbridge.

Coracle building near the bridge.

The Woodbridge.

The Footbridge.

25. JACKFIELD

In the early 17th century Jackfield was a river port with one of the world's first railways bringing coal down from the pits. There was also a pottery, making drinking mugs. Jackfield ware in the 18th century was a highly vitrified black earthenware decorated with gold flowers. The men who operated Severn trows were an infamous, tough lot, hauling the boats by hand until the towpath allowed horses in 1800, and Jackfield catered for them. There were iron furnaces at Calcutts; the bellows powered by a water wheel on the steep stream which also had two mills. Forges were well known for fine cannon, casts and bored here. Lord Dundonald operated coking ovens and tar kilns, producing pitch and oils used for varnish. John Rose, the master potter, moved his industry to Coalport, across the river, as Reynolds developed it.

In the 19th century the main industry was the manufacture of tiles. The Milburgh Tileries produced over four million tiles a year at one time, but the two most famous factories were those of Maws and Craven-Dunnill both of which exported their products all over the world. For a short time the Craven Dunnill works was converted to use as a brass foundry; now it is the Jackfield Tile Museum. Maws factory is a Craft Centre. A small part of the old factory still produces specialist tiles good enough to replace damaged tiles in, for instance, the Foreign Office and also to design and make tiles for special purposes.

Some of the old houses are still inhabited, though the area is often troubled by landslips. The iron bridge to Coalport carries vehicles under two tons and there is a footbridge too. There are several good inns, including the Woodbridge next to the Coalport bridge. There is now much activity on the river, but using canoes and rafts rather than trows. Janet Collins the children's author, has written some interesting stories using the river as a background.

Maws Craft Centre.

Church of St. Mary the Virgin.

Ketley Schools.

Ketley Hall.

26. KETLEY

A former Vicar of Ketley used to describe himself as 'Vicar of all the Ketleys'. He meant of course that he was responsible not only for Ketley but also for Ketley Sands, Ketley Dingle, Ketley Bank and Red Lake.

The name Ketley probably means 'the forest clearing of the cats' though for a long time it was usually called Coalpit Bank. It was first a clearing in The Wrekin Forest, originally a farming settlement until the worth of its rich iron and coal deposits became worth exploiting. Although the name is Anglo-Saxon, Ketley does not feature in the Domesday Book.

In its great days Ketley was a hive of industry and invention. Glynwed and Aga are still thriving industries and the Shropshire Star is as inventive as any local newspaper can possibly be.

In 1757 Abraham Darby, Richard Reynolds and Thomas Goldney leased land from Earl Gower on the present Glynwed site and built an ironworks. They installed a pumping engine to operate the blast furnaces and by 1806 it was the second largest in Shropshire, and famous world wide. Ten years earlier it was making steam engines and nearby there was a coke hearth which also produced coal tar, pitch and oils. The first successful inclined plane in Britain joined the works to the canal which led to Oakengates.

After the Napoleonic Wars industry in Shropshire declined. Many of the inhabitants lived in squatter cottages, some quite comfortable, with up to a quarter of an acre of garden, but only the remarkably handsome Ketley Hall remains. This is still a fine building, parts of which are 400 years old.

William Reynolds may well have been the inventor of the first railway engine, though it had problems which had not been overcome by the time Trevithick built his model at Coalbrookdale. When Shropshire led the world in industry, Ketley was one of its most progressive areas, mainly through the inventions of the Reynolds family of Ketley Hall, but also because they were supported by an able and skilful workforce. At the hall the Reynolds family kept a fine collection of fossils, particularly of the carboniferous period. There were happy to show these to visitors, though not so happy if their guests strayed into the laboratories and workshops where their many inventions were being developed.

The Aga works, on the north side of the Holyhead Road, was founded by James Clay, who moved his agricultural implement business from Foundry Road, Wellington. He amalgamated with the Sinclair works across the road and others to form Allied Ironfounders which eventually became Glynwed.

Modern Ketley still has industry and is well supplied with sporting and leisure facilities but there are few old houses and it seems to lack a centre. Meanwhile Ketley remains a thriving industrial village and its inhabitants still retain the industriousness and skill of their ancestors.

Glynwed Foundry and Reynolds House.

Bank House.

Queenswood School and Telford Centre.

27. KETLEY BANK

Formerly know as Coalpit Bank, Ketley Bank was in the mining business from the beginning of the exploitation of the East Shropshire Coalfield. Its most prominent inhabitant in the 17th and early 18th century was Richard Hartshorne of Bank House, who was a contemporary of Abraham Darby I and of much higher social and business standing, for he was the leading Shropshire coalmaster of his day. It was Hartshorne who sold iron ore, coal and coke to Darby. He had another house which was in Wellington. This may have been the Old Hall, formerly known as Watling Street House.

Richard Reynolds was another well-known character who lived at Ketley Bank. He was a Quaker ironmaster from Bristol and married Abraham Darby II's daughter Hannah; their son William was born here in 1758. The Reynolds family were partners of the Darbys in the Coalbrookdale Company and had many enterprises of their own, such as the development of Coalport and the building of steam engines.

There are still a few old houses mixed among the new in Ketley Bank and it retains a feeling of community. It was once centred on Main Road and surrounded by fields but now all this has changed. Main Road has been cut through by Mossy Green Way and no longer connects to Red Lake. To the south is the M54 and Queensway is a barrier on the east. In fact the new roads have made Ketley Bank far less accessible than it was.

There is a council estate to the east with the street names First, Second, Third, Fourth, Fifth and Sixth Avenue.

Fortunately the inhabitants are more interesting than their addresses. The old Greyhound Inn has survived and given its name to an interchange between the Holyhead Road and Queensway as well as Greyhound Bank. The present state of Ketley Bank is of a village with an expanded population but restricted in area and access by four busy main roads.

Lawley Farm.

Playing Fields and clock.

28. LAWLEY

The small industrial/farming village of Lawley stands at the top of the Dawley Road from Wellington, and is, as I write, in a state of turmoil which has been going on for some time. It is on the coalfield and has been mined for centuries. The useful coal and iron seams ran out and the village reverted to agriculture but in the 1980s a large area has been open-cast mined in preparation for housing and factory development. Soon the parish will be much more densely populated.

The community until recently has been stable and tightly knit. Opposition to the disruption was well organised and well supported but faced the combined forces of Telford Development Corporation (with Whitehall support) and British Coal, Lawley will not be the same again. The new recreation ground and clock are a monument to village unity.

Laveli — Lafa's — Leah — a clearing in The Wrekin Forest, the holding of a Saxon called Lafa, was held by Erngeat before Domesday, but was waste (it's not new!). There was half a hide of land which paid tax; enough land for one plough. William Pandolf, a leading follower of Earl Roger Montgomery held it in Wrockwardine Hundred.

The Shropshire Village Book tells interesting stories of old customs surviving from the days when the inhabitants of Lawley were part pagan. These include 'Soling' on Shrove Tuesday — knocking on doors, begging for pancakes and nailing a hot cross bun to the rafters for a year's good luck. Easter Monday and Tuesday were favourite days — 'Eaving Days' — when boys were entitled to grab girls and heave them off their feet. It sounds fun!

Within the parish of Lawley was an interesting experiment in industrial development called New Dale which has disappeared before the bulldozers. This is dealt with separately.

St. John's Church.

From Dawley Bank, across the Common.

The Common from Old Park.

29. LAWLEY COMMON

It was usual for villages to have a piece of common land until the last few centuries and many of the villages of Telford had such an area. Here the commoners could graze their beasts, hold archery contests and so on. But only bona fida villagers had such rights and these were controlled by the lord of the manor. Most of the village commons disappeared long ago due to the 'tidying up' of land ownership usually called enclosure. By the time many counties were sponsoring parliamentary bills to regulate enclosure a great deal of Shropshire was already decided. Lawley Common has not been in communal ownership for a very long time.

Although this was agricultural land it had coal, ironstone and clay under the surface; these were soon worked out by the technology available. More recently the mineral deposits have been extracted by opencast mining on behalf of the Coal Board and much of the land is now replaced and grassed. That makes it a prime tarket for development, which is scheduled to take place in the latest plans for Telford by Wrekin District Council.

In 1990 and 1991 there have been preparatory roadworks, rerouting the Wellington-Lawley-Coalbrookdale road (A5223) and building new roads to Telford Centre and the M54. The resulting archepelago of islands has caused some consternation whilst building took place. The land north of Station Road, which has a few old houses, is intended for the new Polytechnic of Shropshire, the coming of which has had great support, but a counter-suggestion to site this at Priorslee seems more likely.

South of Station Road the plans are for housing, mainly in the north and east, with employment (presumably industry) in the west, near Wellington Road. The fields lie empty, waiting to see what will happen. It remains to be seen whether the large block of houses proposed in the east will be an extension of Dawley Bank or become a new village of Lawley Common.

The Wrekin from Lawley Common.

The Watermill and Mill Farm.

'Woodhenge'.

30. LEEGOMERY

Modern Leegomery is made up of new (1970-1990s) houses of varing sizes from local council houses and starter homes to large and expensive 'executive' houses. Its most outstanding building is the large Princess Royal Hospital in Apley park, full of modern 'high tech' equipment under its huge red umbrella roof. This was the culmination of many years of campaigning since the 1950s. The other big building is the Japanese Maxell factory, standing starkly and boxily, producing sound and video tapes for Europe, It provides employment which perhaps excuses its ugliness and its use of good agricultural land.

One would not expect to find much history here, but the Saxon settlement of Lee was, before 1066, a clearing in the forest which in 1167 belonged to a Norman called Alfred de Cambrai and added the 'gomery' to its name.

To find anything earlier than new town buildings is not impossible. The old mill has been refurbished in 1991 as an interesting house, leaving some of the machinery in place. Its farmhouse is also modernised. Part of the old Leegomery farm and buildings are now the Thomas Telford pub and the community centre.

Most of Leegomery belonged to Apley estate and was acquired by the development corporation for building. There is a variety of styles and most are attractive. The worst part is the numbering system in some streets which can only have been devised to confuse. Private building has flourished to make a good mix of homes. Shops, schools and some play areas are provided. It is all in the parish of Hadley, though originally, like Hadley itself, it was part of Wellington.

Mill Workings.

Thomas Telford.

Wooden house.

'A' frame house.

31. LIGHTMOOR

Once a place of brickworks, mines, furnaces, foundries, engineering works and pit and slag mounds, Lightmoor is now a fascinating mixture of old and new, of industry and housing, of development and gentle decay. There are controversial plans for its renewal and integration in to the brave new world of Telford, but these are meeting with resistance from Lightmoor's inhabitants, who can be very vocal when they feel the need.

Underneath it all are coal measures, shallow to the west, but east of the Lightmoor fault they are deeper. Consequently the western section was mined first and the eastern part had to wait for deep mining techniques and capital for machinery. There is also clay of the kind which makes firebricks, a very useful commodity. Much of the surface, which now looks very natural, is artificial; mounds of slag or pit refuse, covered with the unique ecology which develops when old industry is recolonised. Left alone it will gradually return to the forest which is the natural vegetation here.

There were three blast furnaces here, three brick and tile works and from 1790 engines were made. One of the brickworks, which made fire bricks until 1984, is still manufacturing but has changed to blue facing bricks. There are still industries in Lightmoor.

There are still houses too; some of the older ones of brick or stone (or a mixture of both) remain, including 'squatter cottages', cottage rows and the unique Lightmoor Project in Leasowes Green. This is a remarkable self-build scheme which has produced some interesting ideas, some of which have been copied in other places. Around the green are substantial new houses of determined individuality built by pioneers, many of whom lived in old caravans while the work went on. Several families work at or from home, often by using modern computer technology. Perhaps the Lightmoor project points the way modern villages will develop.

Bulldozer on site

Holy Trinity Church.

Castle Mound from churchyard.

32. LITTLE DAWLEY

South of Dawley's Holy Trinity Church lies Dawley Parva, more usually called Little Dawley. It is a compact village of housing estates and individual houses, having a couple of shops (one a Post Office, the other a take-away) as a centre. It is not planned for expansion, but to be almost surrounded by the 'green network' which seems the best idea in planning Wrekin Council has had. This not only enables communities to have a breathing space around them but also connects up open spaces with narrow strips, enabling wildlife to move — at night at least.

In 1086 Little Dawley had a villanus, two bordars and a serf; there were woodlands, probably making up much of the land. The 1871 directory lists Little Dawley as a distinct parish, with its church of St. Luke, 'a neat, brick building erected in 1845' (This church was made redundant and sold in 1980). The 1871 population was 2,451; perhaps more than today. There were then seven farmers, two chartermasters, a haulier, two grocers, three innkeepers, two shoe makers, a mining agent, two grocers, a farrier, a blacksmith, a carpenter, a butcher, a relieving officer, the vicar and a registrar of births and deaths. The Coalbrookdale Company made bricks and titles. The above list is very different from the occupations today and shows how much was kept in the village. Modern Little Dawley has to go further afield for these services.

Chartermasters were to mining like tenant farmers are still to their trade. They rented the mining rights and paid rent and royalties to the landowners; they employed labour, paid wages sold coal, iron and clay and hoped to make a profit. The mining agent, however, was paid directly by the owner of the mine as a manager. The only entry without a trade was Mr. Benjamin Edwards of Stony Hill; perhaps he owned land or a mine.

Little Dawley is a continuing village, with its own character, which has changed with the times and will probably continue to evolve.

Old houses in Holly Road.

John Fletcher's iron tombstone.

Figures in the wall of St. Michael's Church.

Upper House Barn.

33. MADELEY

The forest clearing by the Mad Brook — Madeley — is an ancient parish, with a long and fascinating history. It was owned for a very long time by Wenlock Priory and developed into a market town; until the 1970s it was part of the Borough of Wenlock. The octagonal church of St. Michael was rebuilt by Thomas Telford on the site of a pre-Christian mound; its most famous priest was the Swiss John Fletcher, friend and biographer of John Wesley. Fletcher's cast iron tombstone is in the churchyard.

There are fine buildings in Madeley, including the Court House, recently renovated and extended; now a large hotel. This was once a priory farm or grange, enlarged by Sir Robert Brooke, a leading lawyer who became Speaker of the Commons. In the garden is a fascinating astrological sculpture, and opposite the gatehouse is a tree covered spoil mound. A descendant of Sir Robert Brooke built the furnace at Coalbrookdale which became Darby's first. Madeley Court, Abraham Darby and John Fletcher all have schools in Madeley named after them.

The Anstice hall was the first working men's club in England; it also has been well restored and is a community centre for the town. Madeley Hall and its barns are very substantial buildings which have been excellently renovated and added to; the old vicarage too is an historic house. There are several council estates and old cottages. Madeley Educational and Recreation Centre includes Madeley Court School, a theatre, swimming pool and a bowling club; the latter was the first built.

Former inhabitants of note include Thomas Randall, a porcelain manufacturer, and Loud Moulton, a charming man who produced over a million tons of explosives for the War Office after a career at the Court of Appeal. The town was laid out in the middle ages, with 'burgage plots'; long narrow gardens, behind the shops, all of which included living accommodation above and behind.

Modern Madeley is an interesting mixture of old and new buildings, with very little industry left within the town. Its newly formed Parish Council has the largest population of all the parishes in Telford for it includes Woodside, Sutton Hill, Tweedale and Halesfield. There are no plans for any great new developments in Madely itself for no land is available.

St. Michael's Church.

St. Leonard's Church.

The Norman Chapel.

34. MALINSLEE

Another of the forest clearings in The Wrekin Forest, Malinslee took its name from a Saxon woman, Malin. There was a mill in the 14th century, but it was not recorded after 1347. After many centuries of development as an agricultural village there is evidence of exploitation of the minerals by the Eyton family in the early 17th century.

It was Thomas Botfield and his descendants, however, who expanded the industrial potential, first moving coal from Hollinshead, near where the Telford shopping centre is now by rail to Sutton Wharf on the Severn in the late 18th century. By 1840 there were ten deep mines in Malinslee, which is east of the Lightmoor fault, producing coal, iron and clay. The Botfields also had the Old Park ironworks, built in 1790 near the hamlet of Dark Lane. Forges, mills and a third blast furnace were soon added to the original two furnaces, making it the largest in Shropshire. It survived until 1894. Here improvements to chain making were perfected by the manager, Gilbert Gilpin; these were adopted by others in the industry. Nearby was the Old Park brickworks. James Poole of the New Wickets Inn made boilers and nails.

Mainslee, with Little Dawley, was part of the manor of Leegomery from the 13th century and in the 16th century legal matters were decided at Eyton on the Weald Moors. In 1894 it became part of Dawley Urban District, which was abolished in 1974 and The District of The Wrekin Council absorbed it. A parish council was formed in 1988.

There was a Norman chapel which had been disused for some time and was on a site needed for the shopping centre car park. This has been dismantled and erected in the Town Park. St. Leonards church is an octagonal sandstone building, dating from 1805. It closely resembles Telford's Madeley church and it is thought he may have influenced the design.

Although there are some old houses and an inn (The Church Wicketts) near St. Leonards most of Mainslee is now less than twenty years old and the design of both houses and road lay-out have the marks of the development corporation. There is a small shopping centre included in the new development.

The Church Wicketts inn.

Serbian Orthodox Church.

Old house in Muxton Lane.

35. MUXTON

At the extreme north-east of Telford is the village of Muxton. Its name is probably formed from a mixture of Old Welsh — Mochros, meaning swine, — and Anglo-Saxon, tun, a settlement. Its buildings are certainly an interesting mixture of ages. There are timber framed houses, Duke of Sutherland brick houses and several different age/fashions since Elizabethan times without straying from Wellington Road, Muxton.

For much of its life Muxton has been more associated with Lilleshall than with Donnington. Lilleshall had the powerful Abbey and later, as the home base for the Leveson-Gower family empire it became more important still. Since the establishment of the Central Ordnance Depot and even more so since Telford new town was designated Donnington has grown from a small agricultural village to a populous urban sprawl and this has affected its neighbour Muxton.

The Village Book by the Shropshire Federation of Women's Institutes tells an interesting story of Muxton in early industrial days. When the mines and quarries were being worked in Lilleshall, a canal spur lined them to the Marquis of Stafford's canal, running between Pave lane and Donnington Wood. The Lilleshall spur was seventy feet lower than the main canal, so barges were taken into a tunnel where two vertical shafts enabled goods to be raised to the upper canal in box containers. In 1790 the tunnel was abandoned and an inclined plane substituted. For a hundred years this supplied the Lodge Furnaces which produced 'the finest pig iron ever made' and closed in 1888.

The remains of the Lodge Furnace are at the Common, Donnington and at Muxton Bridge are the ruins of a beam engine which pumped water from the mines into the canal. There were two corrugated iron chapels to serve Muxton; one is still used and the other has been transported to Blist's Hill. There is also a brick chapel which is now used by the local Serbian Othodox community who came to Donnington during the second World War. Next to this church is 'Treasure Trove Villas', so called because a hoard of Roman coins was found when the foundations were being dug.

Muxton's buildings include old cottages, modern houses, two hotels and a caravan site. There is much proposed development land including the site of Walker's of Donnington for industry and four large housing sites to the south of the present village.

St. John's Mission Church.

The site of Nash barn from Drummery Lane.

Nash site from Wrockwardine Road.

36. NASH

On the extreme western edge of Telford lies the lost village of Nash. Its loss is not something for which the new town can be blamed in any way for it has been lost for a very long time and there is now little trace of its existence. The medieval township had had a farm in the later 17th century and a single barn in 1839, marked on the first edition Ordnance Survey map, but has been completely deserted for a century at least.

The name Nash means 'at the ash tree' and is quite a common Anglo-Saxon place name. At domesday it was one of the berewicks of Wrockwardine and belonged to the king. Roger Montgomery, Earl of Shrewsbury, was the tenant in chief. The estate of Wrockwardine is said to be of considerable antiquity, perhaps succeding Wroxeter in the fifth century as the administrative centre for the lands of the Cornovii, and later the Wreoken Saetan. It may well be the site of Pengwern.

The site of Nash lies in the middle of fields, half way between Wrockwardine and Orleton, not now connected with the Wrockwardine — Wellington road or with Drummery Lane, even by footpath. There is a small wood, locally known as the tumpy wood, containing several mounds which may well represent house platforms. There seems not to have been any investigation into this area, which may, if and when it is excavated give evidence not only of the lost village but also of much earlier settlement.

It might be assumed that this is another of the casualties of the black death, and this is born out by the 1349 manorial income — nothing — 'because the inhabitants are dead'. However, by 1672 there were three persons paying hearth tax, the same as at Orleton, so there must have been regeneration. Nash is a small mystery which may, some day, be solved.

Looking south-west.

Railway Bridge in Naird Lane.

37. NEDGE HILL

Formerly a part of Shifnal, Nedge Hill and Nedge Farm were included in Dawley New Town and later in Telford. It was planned to be a housing area but this was later abandoned or a least postponed. Current plans include a southwards extension of Stafford Park, industrial development extending right up to Nedge Hill and two new housing areas to the south of the hill.

Nedge Hill, Naird Farm and Dodmoors are all shown on the 1841 OS map as being on the east of the then newly built railway which joined the Shrewsbury and Birmingham line through Coalbrookdale to Buildwas and linked with the Severn Valley and Much Wenlock lines. This railway is still in operation as it provides coal for the power station at Buildwas; there are, however, no passengers or other traffic on the line.

There were proposals floated in the 1980s for a 'Silicon Valley' development to include the whole of Nedge Hill, or at least a sizeable part of it. These plans provoked a great deal of local opposition from the relatively newly arrived inhabitants of Stirchley and Randlay, who stressed the importance of retaining the existing situation and intensifying it into a full-blown nature reserve. Proponents of the 'Silicon Valley' scheme emphasised its non polluting nature and the importance of keeping Telford to the forefront of modern technology.

The present position of Nedge Hill is that the top of the hill has been laid out as a car park and picnic area with some planted woodland to supplement existing trees. Walkways have been made and it is a very pleasant situation. There are excellent views over Telford to The Wrekin and to the Brown Clee Hill. Access is not easy by car — the single track Naird Lane runs from Stirchley Avenue under Queensway and connects with Stafford Park and Shifnal; all the approach roads are narrow. Most of the people who visit Nedge Hill would agree that narrow roads are an advantage.

Looking west.

Open day at Newdale Farm.

Foundations of cottage row.

38. NEWDALE

In the north of Lawley parish the Coalbrookdale Company founded a mining settlement in 1759 with the apparent intention of recreating an industrial village after the manner of Coalbrookdale. By 1794 there were 18 back-to-back houses called the Long Row, with 12 other houses by 1841, when the population was 196. This number changed little until 20th century, when the remaining inhabitants were re-housed by the council.

Recent excavations, just in advance of the opencast working, have made it clear that this was an experiment in new town planning which did not produce the results expected. The two large buildings were factories; a foundry and a forge. A furnace, which should have been powered by the nearby stream and received iron, limestone and coal for coking completed the industrial complex. All the raw materials were to hand. One of the factory buildings was converted into a farm and the other was for a time used as a Quaker Meeting House.

Newdale may well have been the earliest housing/industrial building scheme of its kind but it has now disappeared for ever and its site has no trace on the ground since it was ripped out, the underlying coal removed and the surface soil replaced.

The Long Row was condemned as a slum in the 1960s and demolished, though in its time it was regarded as a revolutionary improvement in housing provision for industrial workers. The houses were well built, if small, and although they seemed identical there was at least one 'double' house for an overseer. Pig styes were provided and there was a pumped water supply.

The six week long archaeological rescue dig in 1987 revealed many of the features of this unique site to a large number of visitors, though as with any scientific inquiry it raised far more questions than it answered.

The planned development has not yet taken place but a new road has been built from Ketley Dingle interchange to Lawley Common, linking to Telford Centre and the old New Works Lane has been reconstructed as a footpath/cycle track. Empty land awaits its future.

Newdale Lane after site clearance.

Market Street.

Railway bridge.

39. OAKENGATES

For some years Oakengates has been a town rather than a village and it now has its own Town Council. The Urban District Council was absorbed by Wrekin Council in the reorganisation of 1974 and in 1988, after a protracted campaign by several unparished areas within Telford, Parish Councils were formed. Oakengates resolved, as was its right, that it was a town.

At one time there was a notice on the railway bridge announcing proudly that Oakengates was 'The Brightest Little Town In Salop'. The recently published 'Oakengates Book', however, shows the town to be more concerned with the inequities of the industrial system and, although its old photographs are excellent, it paints a very gloomy picture of the past.

The meaning of the name Oakengates is obvious, though where the gates were is not known. Were they, perhaps like Haygate, an entrance to The Wrekin Forest? Until the mid 19th century Oakengates was a much smaller place than Wombridge or St. Georges; its growth was probably due to the railway station — now alas only an unmanned halt. The shopping centre grew rapidly in the late 19th and early 20th century to supply the needs of the miners and industrial workers and their families. Its prosperity varied according to the work available, but the two local ironworks, Maddock's and the Lilleshall works at Snedshill closed only recently (1987 and 1959).

There was once a complicated traffic concentration near Snedshill, the main line railway, canal, branch line, works railway and several roads all coming together. Oakengates was famous for cock fighting, bull baiting, drunkenness and non-conformist Christianity at the same time. Oakengates wakes week was well known and at times infamous. The local Co-op was centred here and at one time was a very thriving business. Once there a coffee palace, though it became a labour exchange and was demolished by TDC. Many of the old established shops have gone since the bypass turned the town centre into a traffic island. The Town Hall, at which venue have performed many artists of international repute was in 1991 renamed Oakengates Theatre; this has a large hall, though the accoustics have been criticised. It was built by the UDC and inherited by Wrekin Council.

Oakengates is having to come to terms with its reduced position as a shopping centre caused by the proximity of Telford shopping mall and the restriction of the one-way ringroad. There has also been a breakaway movement; St. Georges and Priorslee have a separate parish. But Oakengates people are resilient; they will make the best of it; there is reason to be more optimistic for the future than the Oakengates Book suggests.

Walker Institute and Technical College.

Chapel, Park Lane.

40. OLD PARK

Until the latter part of the 18th century Old Park was a mainly agricultural estate, though under the soil were useful deposits of iron and coal. Isaac Hawkins Brown, who owned the estate, employed Thomas Botfield as manager and he built the ironworks which led to the formation of the Old Park Company. It became the largest in Shropshire and the second largest in England, with houses for workmen, four blast furnaces and a rolling mill. Botfield, the son of a collier, became an extremely wealthy man and passed on the business to his son. The firm, however, was bankrupt in the 1880s and closed.

By the 1980s Old Park consisted mainly of the spoil mounds of the mines and looked very derelict. The only habitations remaining from the old days are along Park Lane; a few old cottages, a chapel and some newer houses. In 1990 Telford Centre was enlarged westwards to take in most of the Old Park estate and several large superstores including Sainsbury's built, together with their car parks and service roads. In 1991 a further commercial expansion was planned and the City Technology College being built.

In this area there have been many mines of varying depths and types. Before the current building took place it was necessary to drill extensively to check the state of the land below the surface, for most of the mining had been done long before it was thought necessary to make any permanent records of the area and depth of either shafts or galleries. Telford Development Corporation have found and dealt with (sealed) 1,400 shafts but there are few who would deny that there may be others which have not been found in spite of the diligence of the searches.

So Old Park has gone through the phases so often seen in this area; agriculture with a little mining on a small scale, sudden expansion to a nationally important industrial complex followed by collapse of the main firm and a gradual decline, then very recently a rejuvenation as part of Telford Centre. How long this will last is not predictable as some of the new businesses are feeling the current recession.

View from mound.

Orleton Hall.

The Gatehouse.

41. ORLETON

'The tun of the earls' is said to be the meaning of Orleton's name. It has been suggested that the site of Orleton Hall has a very romantic origin — that it was the Great Hall of Cyndyllan, the last Celtic Prince of the Cornovii, or of Powys, who was defeated by Saxons and is commemorated by the poem of Llwarch Hen. This, however, is not proved.

In the 14 century it had a mill, but not for long. There must have been a settlement of some sort — a village or at least a hamlet — to supply the manor for what is clearly a manor house but it had disappeared by the early 18 century. There are some interesting mounds to the south of the house but they seem not to have been investigated.

Ralph of Orleton appears in documents of 1141-55 but the first mention of the manor as such is with Adam who died in 1305. Ownership passed to the Cludde family and then the Herberts, the last two being Earls of Powis, to the present owner, Mr. V.M.E. Holt.

The medieval manor house stood in a square moat, a small part of which still remains, crossed by a stone bridge with two arches. The timbered gatehouse is 16th century on earlier foundations. The oldest part of the house is the inner hall, which is timber framed. The rest is of various dates, remodelled in the 18th and 19th centuries. There are various outbuildings, including stables, a dovecot and a walled garden containing an 18th century gazebo called the bothy.

King Charles I mustered his army in the park here and made a great speech, promising much to his soldiers. Had he kept his promises he would probably have kept his head. It has been claimed that here began the civil war. Since then there has often been a military presence at Orleton; a Major Cludde led the Yeomanry on several occasions, and the last two members of the Herbert family to live there were both colonels. There is also a strong connection with cricket; the local club plays in the park.

Until recently Orleton owned considerable land in Wellington, especially on the west side. One part of Haygate Road was formerly called New Town (near the Haygate Inn, which replaced the Bull Inn, New Town). It has been suggested that the hamlet of Orleton was transferred here. Meanwhile Orleton is, and seems likely to remain, a manor house without a manor.

The Bothy.

The Wrekin from Overdale.

Post Office.

42. OVERDALE

Now mainly a large council estate, Overdale overlooks Newdale, the site of the new town attempt of the Coalbrookdale Company. The soil is nearly all formed from boulder clay, dating from the last Ice Age. Underlying this clay are the Middle Coal Measures, highly complicated by numerous faults. These have long been exploited, not only for coal but also for the iron ore and clay in the seams.

The coal and iron were used at the nearby Ketley works which is still operating under the ownership of the Glywed Company; it was formerly run by the Reynolds family, later by the Coalbrookdale Company and more recently was known as Sinclair's Foundry (it is still called either Sinclairs or The Allied). The factory has always produced 'rainwater goods' — guttering and piping — though some of its output is now in plastic rather than cast iron. These have long been exported as well as supplied for the home market.

Overdale is now cut off from the rest of Ketley by the M54; access to the north is restricted to Rock Road, which passes under the motorway and Gafield Road which connects by an overpass to Mannerley Lane. The new 'Wellington Park' retail park will be so difficult to reach that most of Overdale's shopping will still be done in Wellington or Telford Centre. Although there are plans for the expansion of The Rock and a whole new village at Newdale, Overdale will probably remain much the same for some years.

M54 at Overdale.

Priorslee Hall.

Refurbished old cottages.

43. PRIORSLEE

The forest clearing of the Prior (of Wombridge), Priorslee was for many years part of the parish of Shifnal. From the 18th century, however, it became more and more connected with Oakengates and its industrial development; consequently it was included in Oakengates UDC and remained until most of Telford was unparished in the 1974 reorganisation. In 1988 it was incorporated into St. Georges and Priorslee parish following strong public pressure not to be in Oakengates.

Priorslee Hall was, since the early 19th century, the headquarters of the Lilleshall Company; it was bought by Telford Development Corporation in 1963 and was its head office until 1990, when the corporation moved to New Town House. At the time of writing the hall is scheduled as a grade II listed building and may become the centre for the Polytechnic in Shropshire, though there is opposition from some residents. The sheds which served TDC workers contrast with the fine old building.

There was much mining and many parts of Priorslee are covered in pit mounds; there are two flash pools. Past industries include bricks and tiles, chemicals, coke, concrete, engineering, lime, slag and office equipment as well as iron and coal. Now there are the large factories of Ricoh and NEC and an industrial estate with many small and medium sized units on the site of the demolished Lilleshall Company complex.

There are the remains of the old village, including Stone House, the Lion Inn, several large Victorian houses and a row of fine renovated miners' cottages. New buildings have created an interesting village, some along a 'wharfage' round the pool, others in groups and a new hotel on a high mound which had only just been made a nature reserve. Many of the latest houses are quite expensive 'executive' homes.

Part of the future of Priorslee depends on the question of whether the Polytechnic in Shropshire is allowed to find its home here.

St. Peter's Church.

Community Centre.

The Primary School.

44. RANDLAY

Until the works closed in the 1960s Randlay was well known as the source of exceptionally fine red facing bricks. The factory was established by the Botfields in 1838 and the chimney stands proudly in the town park as a landmark as well as a monument to local industry. Negative traces of the brick trade are represented by Randlay Pool and Blue Pool, formed in the ground from which the clay was extracted. These pools are a major feature of the town park and are home for much wildlife.

The modern Randlay consists mainly of a development corporation estate; this learned from earlier sites and had its shopping and community centre, including a pub and a primary school on the perimeter road, Randlay Avenue, rather than in the middle where it would have been less accessible. The centre is well developed and the school excellent.

Two new private estates are to the west, adjoining the town park, linked to the centre by an underpass. Some of the new houses are of stone and in an interesting 'old fashioned' style; perhaps when they are fully mature they will be thought to be Victorian. Randlay has many footpaths linking its roads and to the centre and the park, yet addresses are easier to find than on many Telford estates. The Green Network is well developed here, encouraging wildlife movement throughout the modern village. Further housing development is planned in four areas to the east, along Stirchley Avenue.

The Randlay valley, the ancient boundary between Dawley and Stirchley, is now the Town Park. Here are a great variety of wild life inhabitants, including the unique ecology which is associated with recolonised industrial sites. This in itself varies as between slag heaps, lime workings, coal mounds and brick working or clay pits. It is to be hoped that the authorities will resist the urge to 'tidy up' this area; if this happens the fragile ecology will be lost.

Randlay Brickworks chimney.

Telford's Mark at Limekiln Bank Roundabout.

45. RED HILL

Probably the oldest established site of human occupation in the Telford designated area, Red Hill's history is either long past or in the future. It was a small first century Roman military installation, apparently surrounded by a later civil settlement, where Watling Street crossed the summit of a hill; probably here is Uxacona, named in the Antonine Itinery. Nearby there is evidence of older use during the Iron Age, but it seems not to have been used in post-Roman times.

The name Red Hill refers to the underlying rock; to the east this is Enville beds — carboniferous brick-red sandstones — and the Permian Lower Mottled or Bridgnorth sandstone, also red, on the western side. Under these rocks are coal measures which have been exploited by deep mining, there being Grange, Lodge and Granville collieries nearby. The land was owned by the Leveson-Gower family since the Reformation. To the north of Red Hill are pit mounds from the deep mines which are being levelled in 1991, preparatory to development.

Most of Red Hill has been farmed continuously since the Iron Age, probably most intensively when it had to provide for the Roman marching camp and its attendant settlement. There is a reservoir on the top; water is pumped up and gravity fed to households below. The road island at Snowhill on the A5 has had a model of Thomas Telford's mason's mark erected in the middle.

Future development is proposed for industry. Wrekin Council's Local Plan for Telford has a large area designated for 'employment' — most of the land north of the A5 — whilst to the south there is to be a substanial housing project in Priorslee. Apart from the Ketley Dingle/Newdale development it is around Red Hill in the east that Telford seems most likely to expand its population.

Eastwards along the Roman Road.

Church gates.

St. Mary the Virgin church.

46. RED LAKE

Begun as a squatter settlement in the 18th century, the mining village of Red Lake has a surprisingly rural feel about it. The name almost certainly comes from one of three pools which powered local furnaces; these contained a heavy pollution of iron oxide (rust) from the iron ore, and so were red. Near the edge of the M54 was Cow Wood, where pits were worked within living memory; most of Red Lake has been mined for coal in small shallow pits, for the coal was near the surface, and there was no need for sophisticated technology.

Red Lake was within the Lilleshall estate of the Leveson-Gower family, who tolerated the squatters as they provided the local labour force. In 1812, however, James Lock became the estate manager and made cottagers pay rent, destroyed unsafe houses, repaired others and loaned money to 'good' families to buy a cow and grazing land. Some houses, such as Shrubbery Cottage, were enlarged and redesigned in 'Duke of Sutherland' style.

The early Victorian church of St. Mary the Virgin is a fine example; it was built at a cost of £1,300 to the second Duke of Sutherland, in grey stone with a pyramid roof on its tower. The red brick vicarage stands in grounds with mature trees, one of several Victorian villas, spaced between old cottages, many of which have been extended and modernised. There are also some modern infill houses and bungalows, many of which were built on the fields where the original cottagers' cows grazed.

Modern Red Lake has a feeling of maturity and is a pleasant place to live, even it if is down wind of the Ketley works. To the north is the Holyhead Road, with Mossy Green Way to the east and the M54 on the south. Access to Ketley Town in the west is by footpath only, across open pitmound country which is returning slowly to the forest which was here before coal became so important. Unfortunately there are plans to build houses on some of this land.

Stone wall, Shepherds Lane.

Quarry House Inn.

Old School (now Youth Club), Gower Street.

47. ST. GEORGES

The original name, Pains Lane, has now disappeared from the map of Telford, but there are still local people who refer to St. Georges by that name. In the 1980s there was a strong 'grass roots' movement to create parishes within Telford where the old Urban District Councils had been abolished, leaving no scope for the expression of the individuality of settlement. Nowhere was that so strong as in St. Georges, who were determined not to be in part of Oakengates as they had been for a century. After a long campaign, honour was satisfied and the present council is St. Georges and Priorslee.

The name clearly comes from the large and interesting church of St. Georges, provided by funds from Isaac Hawkins Browne on land donated by Granville Leveson-Gower, second Marquis of Stafford. Browne was a local landowner and had mining interests. This is Lilleshall country, as shown by street names; Gower Street, Stafford Street, Granville Street, Duke's Way, Place and Street. Opposite the church is the Quarry Inn, whose sign is most noteworthy. There are also the Church Institute and the Recreational Club, the latter set in playing fields.

The first edition 1" Ordnance Survey map shows St. Georges or Painslane as a larger and more important place than Oakengates; but that was before the railway with its large station at Oakengates had made such a difference to the siting of the shops. Before the railway, shopping was done by horse and trap or on foot, but when there were frequent stations it became more usual to take the train. The shopping centre affected the district boundaries and St. Georges joined Oakengates. Now both railway and shops have been upstaged by Telford Centre.

The old Roman road is now Albion Hill, West Street, Church Street and Limekiln Bank, where it has been severed from the A5, the easterly section, near the road island on which is Telford's mason's mark. Housing is varied from small cottage rows to large expensive houses; old, new and modernised, which makes for a pleasant mix of population. Additional housing is planned for the north and east, with some land scheduled for mineral extraction between the two. There is a strong community sense, well expressed by the Parish Council.

St. George's Church.

Shawbirch Farm.

Pool at Rough Pits.

48. SHAWBIRCH

At the crossroads of the ancient Portway and the north/south road through Wellington, stood for well over a hundred years, Shawbirch Farm. It looks as though it is able to provide some comfort for travellers as well as act as the base for a considerable acreage. The house has three bays and is three storeys including dormers; it is of good red brick and has still a large barn to match.

The land here is glacial sand and gravel and would be easy to plough even with light tools used before the Iron Age; underneath is sandstone, like the rest of the north Shropshire plain. To the north are the Weald Moors, and this area is really a part of the moors, though being better drained it was probably not part of the lakes which developed after the ice age. The name Shawbirch probably comes from the Anglo-Saxon scarga, meaning 'small wood', which makes the translation 'The place of the small birch wood'. Just north of the farm was 'Rough Pits', a piece of land which has been used as a well designed pool and wood 'amenity area', visually enhancing the place and providing for some wild life and dog walkers.

The recent history of Shawbirch is that a TDC estate for rent was completed in 1982 and this was followed by houses for sale, mostly detached neo-Tudor. The notorious crossroads (I have the scars) was made a little safer by an island. Plans to turn the farmhouse into a restaurant/bar were refused both by WDC and the Ministry; it is hoped that the building will not be lost, as it is the only old structure around. The late 1980s housing boom resulted in an expansion of 'private sector' building and there is now quite a village here.

By the 1990s a new inn has been built, some shops and a primary school. These, together with the community centre and medical centre are sufficient facilities for a village — in fact many long established villages would envy them. The question is, however, how long it will take for the people of Shawbirch to create that sense of social cohesion which makes them into a true village. Their unity in opposing the plans to convert the old house suggests this may not take so long.

Pool with The Wrekin in background.

Trading Estate and Greyhound Interchange.

Construction in Enterprise Zone.

49. SNEDSHILL

A wooded hill, between Wombridge and Prioslee parishes, Snedshill has flourished as an industrial centre since it was owned by John Wilkinson in the 18th century. He installed his 'Topsy-Turvey' engines in both the mines and the furnaces. At the beginning of the 19th century the Lilleshall Company became owners and developed not only a large steel works south of the Holyhead Road but also their brickworks to the north.

In 1959 the tall chimneys of the steelworks were felled by explosives, though many of the workshops are still standing and used for other purposes. The Priorslee Trading Estate and the Castle Trading Estate to the east have a fascinating collection of uses, ranging from a concrete works to a snooker centre. The old giant may be dead and gone but there is still a great deal of activity on the site. Some of the new firms operate in the old buildings but there are also purpose built modern sheds, not of any architectural merit but functional workplaces.

There have been many large and small mines; the sites of some shafts are shown on the Geological Survey map. It is to be devoutly hoped that they have all been located and efficiently capped, for there were many mines here before it was thought necessary to record their positions. The original Sneds Hill has been covered with spoil from mine workings, but it had been recolonised and is now an open space with interesting views.

On the east of the hill is the village, with some old houses around a small green and a few of the workers terraces. Most of the old cottages were thought to be unfit for modern living and were replaced by council houses of much higher standard of comfort if not of visual attraction. The church of St. Peter may have been built for Priorslee but it is in Snedshill now. It is a fine example of early Victorian work.

The brickworks, whose glazed chimneys were a landmark, changed to sanitary ware and produced thousands of glazed sinks and lavatory pans. It is now a 'cash and carry'. There are new industrial and office building overlooking Queensway. Between these two areas is the Greyhound interchange, a complicated junction of roads built on top of the railway tunnel; but not as complicated as it was. In its heyday at this point there were also a branch line railway, a canal junction and a works light railway. So at the same spot were barges, railway trains, works waggons, horses and carts, cars, and vans, lorries, bikes and pedestrians. Fortunately everything went much slower!

The southern part of Snedshill is in the Enterprise Zone, so is expected to expand with industry. There is housing planned in the east. Otherwise Snedshill is likely to remain an interesting village with a very mixed economy.

Central Park.

The Railway Station.

Horsehay Steam Trust Railway.

50. SPRING VILLAGE

Most of Spring Village is just to the north and west of Horsehay Pool, beyond which was for well over a century the Horsehay Works. The present village is much quieter than it was when the works was producing its bridges, girders and cranes. Or rather it was until 1991, when opencast working was introduced in the northern part of the village land. Many of the houses are of high quality, bought in the expectation of peace and quiet, and the inhabitants were understandably upset by the prospect of the huge diggers and earth movers needed for the working.

There is a long row of good quality cottages on the west side of the pool which have been renovated and modernised with care. These give some historical perspective to the village, most of which is new. There has been much thought given to the pool itself and the surrounding area which has been planted to encourage wildlife and to make an attractive background for the village. By 1840 the village was an area of many miners' cottages, most of which were very hastily and inexpertly built and had to be repaired or demolished and rebuilt. It is very different now.

The Horsehay Steam Trust has a railway through the village from the Horsehay Pool to Heath Hill. This line once brought iron ore and coal to the works from Dawley, but it is now used for pleasure only. In the last century there was also a light railway track from the Limekiln Woods, as the furnaces at Horsehay needed lime as flux for the making of pig iron from iron ore.

At various times there have been nonconformist chapels at Spring Village, though never a church. There is now a village hall on Bridge Road in the southernmost corner of the village. Future plans show small housing developments in the south and north west, but it seems the planners' intention to leave the central area, Lawley Common, as open green space.

Concrete Spire.

Looking east.

51. STAFFORD PARK

The large industrial estate of Stafford Park has no houses at all, though there is some dormitory accommodation at the Fire Station. Yet it is designed on very similar grounds to the early housing estates for the Development Corporation, having an outer ring road, Naird Farm Road, which contains the estate. Its other boundaries are the M54 on the north and Queensway (A442) on the west.

Within these are service roads which are numbered, so that, in theory at least, it is easy to find any business from its address. Many of the firms which operate here are nationwide rather than local, and a great variety of goods is manufactured, processed or distributed; consequently there is a large volume of heavy traffic, much of which uses the Castle Farm Interchange (Junction 4) of the motorway. In 1991 a part of Stafford Park is the temporary home of The Polytechnic in Shropshire, a very welcome facility for the country. Yet the estate is surprisingly quiet even on busy days and it is extremely difficutlt to find anyone from whom to inquire the way. The Naird roundabout on Naird Farm Road has a concrete spire, a deliberate landmark which has been the target for much local humour unsuitable for publication.

Many of the more prestigious firms have landscaped their buildings. It is hoped this practice will spread, as the structures are themselves, whilst providing a good working environment, hardly likely to attract favourable comment for their architecture. When the trees that are planted mature, and when more are added, there will be a much enhanced feel to the whole project. There is enough local pressure to insist that new industry should plant enough trees to absorb their carbon dioxide gas emissions.

There is a myth, whether deliberately put about or not, that Telford was built on derelict land and old slag tips. It is not true. Stafford Park, for instance, was farm land before 1973, when the services, roads and factories were developed. The agricultural land use map shows the area was good arable and grazing land.

This is not a lost village; there is no trace of a village, but it was not derelict either. Its future depends on many factors, most of which are in Europe and are related to world trade rather than local factors.

Towards Telford Centre from footbridge.

The Lime Kilns.

52. STEERAWAY

The tiny hamlet of Steeraway is at the top of Limekiln Lane, just before it enters the woodlands. It consists now of only a farm and a few houses but has been a very busy place in its time. The lane is probably ancient as it leads to the Bronze Age village at Willowmoor. There is a rich strip of carboniferous limestone from here to Little Wenlock which has been extensively quarried and mined; also on the east there are productive coal seams. The abandoned limestone mines in Limekiln Wood were being made safe in the 1990s and the old track diverted.

Steeraway produced lime for the ironworks and had a light railway — called the ginny rails — to Horsehay works. Lime was also used for agriculture and for this purpose it was burned in the kilns, using coal for fuel. A railway for this extended to Watling Street. The lime working and kilns were last operated by the Steeraway Lime Company whose owners included the Groom and Ison families of Wellington. Previously the owner of the land had been Lord Forester.

The farm was acquired by the coal board and an extensive opencast mining operation in the 1970s removed many thousands of tons of coal from the fields to the north. During this operation a number of small pits were uncovered, including bell pits, some medieval, some dating from the general strike in the 1920s. The remains of the Isolation Hospital, long ago abandoned because the diseases it catered for are almost eradicated, also were removed.

To the south-east the Short Woods were mined for coal; the last private mine in east Shropshire — an adit — was closed in 1970. Below the wood it is honeycombed with mines and an underground fire sent up smoke at intervals throughout the 1970s and 1980s. The northern tip of Limekiln Wood has a reservoir which supplied Wellington from around 1870 but now is only used for fishing.

In Wrekin Council's latest planning proposals the part of Steeraway within the Telford boundaries is scheduled as 'countryside fringe'. We must hope that means it will stay as it is.

Steeraway Farm.

St. James Church.

Stirchley Grange.

53. STIRCHLEY

For the purposes of this article Stirchley is a large area surrounding Brookside on three sides — west, north and east. It includes the old village and new estates west of Brookside Avenue, those to the east around Holmer Lake and the estate between Grange Avenue and Queensway. These are often seen as separate entities in themselves but are interdependent.

There are several schools which were originally First, Middle and Upper schools with some Special provision but have been reorganised to the traditional Infant, Junior and Secondary modes. Primary schools include Holmer Lake and Birchbank, with the former Upper School now the Lord Silkin School. Tertiary education, as in all Telford, is at New College, Wellington.

Stirchley as a community is well provided for, with a community centre, a library, a youth club and a large recreation centre. There are two small shopping centres, including a post office and a chemist; also a modern church replacing the attractive church of St. James, now redundant. The old Stirchley Grange, once owned by Buildwas Abbey, is on the edge of the Town Park. Part of this building is an Environmental Interpretation Centre, with Countryside Wardens and courses run by Birmingham University; the rest is a garden centre.

Stirchley village is the old pre-industrial centre, and from here developed the industries which were to flourish in the 18th and 19th centuries. Thomas Botfield was one of the local prime movers, together with Isaac Hawkins Browne. Stirchley Hall is a fine building which has been renovated along with its stone barns, making a delightful housing complex.

Holmer Lake is a reservoir around which three housing estates have been built, including starter homes and 'executive' housing, with two schools and a pub. There is quite good provision of open space in most of the area, including playing fields, and there are numerous footpaths throughout the modern village.

Stirchley had been at least three different villages; agricultural, industrial and its modern self, which is mainly a residential part of Telford. Future plans are for minor infilling of houses; these will lessen the amount of open space for the public and increase the demand for it.

Stirchley Hall.

Madebrook House.

Day Centre.

54. SUTTON HILL

The first housing estate of the Development Corporation, Sutton Hill, was designed on two firm principles; there was to be high density but not high rise buildings. To keep the rents within the capacity of the tenants the houses had to be built at the lowest cost possible. In the event houses were being built for sale at the same time in other parts of what is now Telford for less cost for the same accommodation. The reason for this has not been satisfactorily explained.

Most of the new tenants came from the West Midlands conurbation and were well used to high density living. This was an open field site and enjoyed pleasant views over the surrounding countryside, though to the north Madeley had been extended by its Hills Lane estate, some of the facilities of which were useful to Sutton Hill people. A later extension to the south, called Sutton Heights, includes much larger and more expensive houses on the edge of the Great Hay golf course.

The estate proper is enclosed within Sutton Way, with access roads (all with names beginning with S) to the houses and the local centre. The latter includes a Pastoral Centre, Primary School (Alexander Fleming), Scout and Guide HQ, Community Arts, Play Centre, post office and community centre; the village is very well provided for. It is not easy for a stranger to find the way into this complex, however.

Off Sutton Way, Great Hay Drive leads to the Telford Hotel Golf and Country Club at Hay Farm, where Abraham Darby III lived in style from 1771 to his death in 1789. Much renovated and extended it provides excellent facilities.

Apart from agriculture the Sutton Hill area provided spring water for parts of Ironbridge in the 18th century. There was no village before Telford but there certainly is one there now. The development corporation built 1,233 houses in the ancient parish of Sutton Maddock between 1966 and 1969. Some have been sold off very cheaply, others on the 'right to buy'. Yet others have developed such faults — sometimes due to vandalism — that they have had to be demolished and replaced. But many Sutton Hill houses are still happily inhabited by their original occupants.

Sutton Hill Community Centre.

Newly refurbished shopping mall.

Looking from Play Area.

55. TELFORD CENTRE

The busy, bustling shopping and administrative centre of Telford could hardly be described as a village, but like most of the area there was life here before, so it has been included in 'Lost Villages'. Planned as the centre for Dawley New Town, it sparked off not a little antagonism from traders in the old established towns by providing free buses from outside their shops; there were also signs pointing to 'Town Centre' away from the centres of towns. And this at a time when there was only one shop in Telford Centre!

Things are different now, especially as it is growing into more than an American 'out of town' shopping mall. But there are still facilities which any mature town would expect to have which are absent here. There have been moves from Dawley Parish Council and others to have Telford designated as a city, which would require a cathedral in a centre which does not have a conventional church — or even a pub.

The plans were begun in 1964, using the site of Malinslee Hall and the ruined chapel which was repositioned in the Town Park. There was housing in Dark Lane, Spout House and some pits with their attendant mounds, most of which were regenerating in an attractive way. There was also farm land and some of the former inhabitants have expressed their regret for that this has gone to please the newcomers.

There have been several phases and styles of building depending on the current government and the economic climate. At first it was all ugly sheds enclosing the overheated underlit shopping mall full of branches of national High Street firms. This is now in private ownership and a creditable attempt is being made to improve its looks.

The present situation is that the shopping centre has outgrown its rectangular ring road and is spreading into Old Park. The centre's success is directly attributable to the decline in the town centres of Wellington, Oakengates and Dawley and was clearly a deliberate policy of the Development Corporation who spent large amounts of public money to this end.

Recent developments have increased the area's centralisation and provided more facilities at Telford Centre; recreation, administration, transport and legal. Crime has expanded by around 2,000% since 1963 and courts have had to deal with it. The railway has been diverted and what has been called 'the world's ugliest station' competes with 'the worst built motorway'. There have been improvements in building style recently. Perhaps when it has had time to mature the majority of Telford's population, those who were here before it was created, will come to love Telford Centre.

From St. Quentin Gate.

Royal Army Ordnance Corps sentries.

*'Duke of Sutherland' house,
Humbers Lane.*

56. THE HUMBERS

Most of the area known as The Humbers consists of the Central Ordnance Depot, which has been described under Donnington. To the north are two areas belonging to the Ministry of Defence which are the married quarters and barracks for the military personnel responsible for the Depot together with administrative and sports facilities. Most of its life this has been an open area but since threats by the IRA there are barriers and guards.

In times of war — the Falklands or Gulf wars for recent examples — the Depot is very busy indeed, with trains and trucks leaving and arriving at frequent intervals. Between these emergencies, however, it is a remarkably peaceful place for a military base.

Except, that is, when there is a fire. There have now been three huge disastrous fires which have cost the taxpayer hundreds of millions of pounds. None of these fires has been explained to the public, who are left with the assumption that either there was deliberate sabotage by persons unknown or that there is some gross inefficiency in the command structure. Whatever the cause, it is public knowledge that the precautions recommended after the second fire were not carried out before the third.

Most of the employees of the MOD at Donnington are civilians; civil servants who live locally. Many have served for long periods and it is quite common for two generations of the same family to work here.

A small part of Hoo Farm has been turned into a most interesting nature reserve, with pools, woodland and wild meadows, and provided with a car park. This is new in 1991 and will take some years to mature into its full potential though the number of bird species is already on the increase.

A large area within Telford to the north of The Humbers is scheduled as 'Countryside Fringe' and it is not proposed to develop here. This land is within the area of the Weald Moors and is of considerable ecological interest.

Hoo Farm Nature Park.

The Rock.

Methodist Church.

57. THE ROCK

By 1794 The Rock and Mannerley Lane were a string of colliers' cottages south of Red Lake. There were pits here long before, and one of the newer roads at The Rock is Bellpit Lane. By 1813 the cottages had spread north around Gorsty (later Cow) Wood to Red Lake. These remained until 1930-36, when 32 council houses were built at Mannerley Lane and The Rock; a further 213 were added in 1948-56, comprising the Overdale estate, and more were added in the 1970s.

Telford Development Corporation planned an estate of over 600 rented and private houses east of The Rock. In the early 1980s some of the private houses had been built; during the building boom of the late 1980s a much larger number were completed and construction is still continuing in the early 1990s, though recession is having an effect. Many of the later houses have been in the south west and Rock Road has been rerouted and improved.

By no means all the produce of local pits was coal; The Rock collieries produced 150 tons of fireclay a week in the 1950s and 1960s and there was more from later opencast mines. William Light owned quarries at The Rock which produced useful carboniferous sandstone, but these had closed before 1892 by the Duke of Sutherland, who now owned them. These quarries may explain the place name.

Until ten years ago The Rock was known only as a small council estate and a few old cottages, in one of which lived a Shropshire Buddhist given to hang gliding from The Wrekin until at seventy he changed to model aeroplanes. It is now a thriving community in new private houses with some further expansion planned for when the economic climate improves.

Rock Road.

Queensway.

Methodist Church.

58. TRENCH

Situated between the parishes of Wrockwardine (Wrockwardine Wood), Wellington (Hadley) and Wombridge, Trench grew up in the 18th and 19th century as an industrial settlement. At first it was concentrated along the Trench Road, with miners cottages, some with sufficient land to keep a cow and grow enough vegetables to provide a surplus for Wellington market. As mining increased, and other industries came, the settlement grew until now it is a mature village filling most of the area available.

Trench is most famous for its inclined plane, of which there is now unfortunately nothing to show. There were canals here in the early 19th century and the incline raised boats from lower to higher ground; locks could have done the job but there would have been so many that the incline was far more efficient. Until the early 1960s it was possible to trace the course of the canal, though it was long disused and filled with vegetation; now it is built over. Trench Pool was used for balancing the canal water levels; nearby is the Blue Pig inn. This pub's official name used to be the Shropshire Arms but it was always called the Blue Pig.

There are five schools — The John Hunt School (named after Lord Hunt of Everest fame), Teagues Bridge School, Wrockwardine Wood C of E School, St. Luke's R C School and Wrockwardine Wood County School. The two Wrockwardine Wood Schools, are frequently confused with The Wrockwardine Wood School, which is in Wrockwardine Wood. Oakengates Leisure Centre, with its associated playing fields is in the south east corner. There are two small shopping centres, a youth club and a community centre.

The old Trench Road has been bypassed and the main A518 traffic now is diverted to the north, which has been a great advantage to local traffic. To the south the roads to Wrockwardine Wood, Wombridge and Oakengates have been cut by the Wrockwardine Wood Way, speeding through traffic at the expense of the locals. Modern Trench is now almost entirely residential, providing skilled labour for all the various industries in the neighbourhood.

Trench Pool.

Russells Rubber Factory.

Blockley's Brick Works.

59. TRENCH LOCK

Whilst Trench is residential, Trench Lock is, apart from a landscaped area around Middle Pool, completely industrial. The largest area is taken up by Blockley's Brick Works, by far the biggest remaining factory of its kind in Telford.

There was a brick and tile works in 1882, immediately south east of Hadley village, which closed before 1901. By then B. P. Blockley had opened the Ragfield Tileries at New Hadley, next to the Coalport Branch railway. The works specialised in blue and red bricks before 1912. Blockleys Ltd. added a third works in 1935; by 1963 the works produced 20,000,000 facing bricks a year, and in 1964 there were 155 employees. Demand fluctuated but there were 500 in 1973 and further expansion in 1980. Pavior bricks are also made there, facilitating pedestrianisation schemes.

Other factories at Trench Lock include Russells Rubber, making parts for the motor industry, British Telecom and Sommerfield. There is also a motor parts supplier on the Trench Lock interchange. There are no traces of the canals or the lock, and even the old canal bridge on the Trench Road has been swept away. The railways too, both the main line from Wellington Junction to Stafford (apart from the private railway to COD Donnington) and the Coalport branch line have long disappeared. There are excellent road communications, as is usual in Telford, and Trench Lock is centrally placed, though the actual exits from the estate could be much better.

There is no housing in Trench Lock; Chestnut Terrace and Kearton Terrace are both really part of Hadley. The futures of the industries there depend upon market trends and both the motor and the building industries are subject to fluctuation. The area south of Blockleys supplies clay and its future depends on the outcome of the S. E. Hadley planning brief, which will consider mineral extraction.

Middle Pool.

The Cuckoo Oak.

Tweedale Industrial Estate.

60. TWEEDALE

Before Telford there was no such place as Tweedale; there was, however, the Cuckoo Oak and the 1808 map shows Cuckoo-oak Gate. This was an area around the Cuckoo Oak pub on the crossroads, and it is a name which has survived in spite of all the odds. The crossroads has been completely re-aligned with a large island, the houses are gone and the pub has been demolished; yet the name lingered on as the electoral ward and a fine new pub has been built near the old site, so there is a Cuckoo Oak again.

Near the Cuckoo Oak are the fire and ambulance stations for South Telford with access to the A442 Brockton Way and easy connections to the major road network. Along Kemberton Road in the south are miners' cottages, much improved from the old days. To the west is a wooded site for camping and caravans. The Queensway/Brockton Way junction in the north-east obliges drivers heading north to pass under the road they came on.

Madeley Court mines were worked for some seventy years from 1840 when James Foster exploited coal and iron, letting it to charter masters. All the spoil heaps south of the court had been planted by 1901 and production ceased by 1910. In 1845-6 Foster built three blast furnaces near the mines, replacing his Wombridge plant, bringing workmen with the factory. Madeley Court pig iron supplied his works in Staffordshire and Worcestershire. The ironworks was taken over by Thomas Parker, an electrical engineer, in 1912; he established Court Works Ltd. which for seventy years supplied iron casting for the electrical industry.

The Court Works has been converted into an industrial estate shared by several firms. A purpose built estate, Tweedale has been provided by the Development Corporation which consists of large steel framed buildings clad in grey sheeting and houses a variety of factories. To the south are three groups of houses with some small industries. The west side has Madeley Court itself, now a very well appointed hotel, and the Court School with its integrated Recreation Centre, surrounded by woods, playing fields and lakes.

Ambulance and Fire Stations.

Watling Street from the Cock to the Buck's Head.

The Old Hall.

61. WATLING STREET or WELLINGTON HAY

Only the name of the street itself, a section of what was the old A5, now 'detrunked' and named, but not usually called the B5061 remains of the ancient settlement of Watling Street. Even that is not its original name, for it was called Wellington Hay — a Royal deer enclosure — when King John excluded it from his grant to Thomas of Erdington of Wellington manor.

The manor house of Wellington Hay or Watling Street is now called the Old Hall and has been a school since the last century. Previously it was the seat of the Forester family who began as foresters of Mount Gilbert or The Wrekin forest and became major landowners in Wellington, Dothill, Little Wenlock and Willey. The fifth baron sold most of the land and the house early this century. In 1934 half became part of Wellington Urban District and in 1966 the southern half was transferred from Wellington Rural parish to Little Wenlock, which gained the section up to the M54 in 1987.

The northern boundary of the manor was the old Roman road, rebuilt by Thomas Telford and until early this century called Street Lane. The hay or deer enclosure to the south explains some local names — Haygate Road, The Haygate, The Wickets (nothing to do with cricket, but a small gate into the hay) and Kings Hay Road.

The Old Hall or Watling Street Hall as it once was, has 17th century timber framed ranges on the north and east sides. Otherwise it has been added to often, especially since it has been a school. Perhaps its most famous headmaster was Dr. Cranage, who was a prime mover in the ecumenical movement though he excluded Roman Catholics.

As a parish Watling Street or Wellington Hay is now gone for ever. The street name, however, exists not only in Wellington, between the Cock Hotel and the Buck's Head, but also in various towns along the road to London and also in Church Stretton.

Holyhead Road (Street Lane).

Market Hall.

Market Square.

62. WELLINGTON

Although entitled by a seven-hundred-year-old market charter to be called a town, Wellington has been included to complete the gazetteer of communities in 'Lost Villages'. The town grew to be the main market, commercial and administrative centre for the coalfield people and for the agricultural area around. Here was the main railway junction and shopping centre, the magistrates' court, and the largest banks and cinemas; Wellington regarded itself as serving east Shropshire in the same way Shrewsbury served the western part. Yet T. Auden's History of Shropshire, the standard work of 1912, did not mention Wellington at all! Perhaps he came from Shrewsbury.

Not now considered as an industrial place, Wellington has had early cloth and leather industries and cast church bells as well as its more recent fame as a centre for agricultural implements, the timber trade, nailmaking, brewing and the manufacture of bread ovens. The largest fat stock market in the country has become a superstore; one of the country's most inventive makers of agricultural tools has been demolished in 1990 to make room for housing. Both the foundry and the timber yard of the largest timber buyers in Britain are now car parks.

Wellington market is a private company and the largest in Shropshire. It has sustained its town through difficult times, especially when trade was being lost to subsidised shops in Telford centre; now it is open four days a week. The market was on The Green, north of All Saints Church before the 1244 charter, when it moved to Market Square until in Victorian times a new hall was built; this site expanded in 1990.

Famous Wellingtonians include Dr. William Withering who discovered digitalis in the late 18th century and Sarah Smith (Hesba Stretton) who sold a million and a half copies of her book *Jessica's First Prayer*. William helped found the anti-slavery movement and Sarah the NSPCC. Schools include New College, the sixth form college for Telford, and Telford College of Arts and Technology as well as five county primaries and three comprehensive secondaries, two Roman Catholic schools and the independent Wrekin College and Old Hall School.

Most of Wellington is residential and there is planned expansion of the 17,000 population. The town centre has been pedestrianised and in spite of Telford shop rents are still high. There are several churches and a mosque, a YMCA, a small theatre, a swimming pool and a very large number of voluntary societies. The constituency Labour and Conservative parties both have their headquarters in Queen Street and there are the offices of many other organisations in the town. Arleston, Dothill and Shawbirch are within its parish boundaries.

Wellington has been described as The Wrekin's own town, and The Wrekin is Wellington's own hill.

Lychgate and The Wrekin from The Green.

St. Mary and St. Leonard Church.

Parkland and Wombridge Way.

63. WOMBRIDGE

Although Wombridge was for many centuries an important monastic centre and until the coming of the railway the main settlement in the area, Oakengates became a shopping centre in the mid 19th century and Wombridge has been reduced to a small suburb. It is now restricted to the northwest of Oakengates, shut in by Wombridge Way and Queensway and can be approached only from Hadley Road and Oakengates.

The monastery owned much land here before the dissolution and had iron mines and foundries. At one time there was a great deal of iron produced and too many trees were being cut for charcoal. This caused a decree limiting the number of trees felled but the iron production remained constant. Some historians have wondered whether the monks had discovered an alternative fuel — perhaps anticipating Abraham Darby — or if perhaps this was merely a case of medieval 'creative accounting'.

Later the Foley family had charcoal furnaces and by the 18th century the Charltons of Apley were mining iron and coal. At the end of that century William Reynolds had a tunnel dug from the Wombridge mines to his blast furnaces at Donnington Wood, a mile and a quarter away. Sand from Wombridge supplied the moulders at the Horsehay ironworks. There were chemical industries here too — in the 1790s to produce sulphuric acid from iron pyrites and later to produce soap, dyes and sodium sulphate, but this ended in 1803. James Foster had two iron smelting furnaces but closed them down in 1834 and moved to Madeley Court with his skilled men, leaving half the parish derelict industrial wasteland.

The old church was demolished in 1869 and the present church of St. Mary and St. Leonard built of rusticated stone. The ruins of the Augustinian priory, which was founded in the 12th century lie below the church; otherwise there are only a few street names (Abbey Road, Priory Road, Abbot's Close and The Cloisters) to remember it by.

Many of the houses in Wombridge were built by the Oakengates UDC or Wrekin Council; they are much more comfortable to live in than the little cottages of the previous century. There are open spaces to the north and east, which are planned to remain as part of the 'Green Network'.

Priory Road.

Woodside from Park Lane.

Community Centre.

64. WOODSIDE

To the west of Madeley town is the Development Corporation estate of Woodside, similar to other housing estates in new towns all over the country. There is high density and low rise as at the earlier Sutton Hill, and provision of 'village centre' facilities. Woodside is enclosed within its main perimeter road, Woodside Avenue, Castlefields Way, Ironbridge Road and Parkway. It is the largest of the TDC estates and 2,420 houses were built between 1968 and 1973.

Before the development there was Rough Park, a collection of houses and squatter cottages along Rough Park Lane, which led from the Madeley-Ironbridge road to Lightmoor, together with a track to Madeley Court. Rough Park Lane is now approximately Park Lane, which goes through the estate but is blocked to through traffic at the village centre. One of the few old houses remaining is Rough Park farmhouse on Woodside Avenue which became a riding school. There are 200 acres of derelict land north and west of Woodside which are now called Rough Park and are used for recreation.

The village centre is well provided with shops, a community centre, a police station, youth club, church centre, play school and Scout and Guide HQ. There are also the Woodside and William Reynolds County Schools; the secondary schools are Abraham Darby, a comprehensive with a particularly good reputation for music across the road to the south and Madeley Court School to the north-east.

All the roads leading into Woodside begin with W, which makes for convenience, though they do not link up, which is less convenient but prevents traffic driving through and is no doubt safer. There are some blocks of flats but most of the accommodation is in three bedroom houses. There have been criticisms of the housing and of the people, but there are many Woodside residents who will fiercely defend their estate from all comers.

Madeley Court and Gate House.

Almshouses.

Boys' School (now a shop).

65. WROCKWARDINE

The ancient village of Wrockwardine was originally proposed as a part of Telford new town but excluded from the final designation. It has been suggested that Wrockwardine was the capital of the Anglo-Saxon territory of the Wreoken Saetan, the 'Wrekin Settlers' who ruled most of the Shropshire and the lands around between the Celtic post-Roman times and the coming of the Mercians. Certainly Wrockwardine was the principal place of the Hundred at Domesday and is of great antiquity.

In the event most of Wrockwardine village was not to be in Telford, though Admaston, which is within the parish, has been very much affected. Those parts of Wrockwardine within the Telford boundaries, this is west of Wellington and the railway, together with Bratton north-west of Bratton Road, have not and are not planned to be built up. So the eastern lands of the village, which originally it was feared would be swamped by rows and rows of brash new houses are still the farmlands they have been for many centuries.

This is not to suggest that the village itself has been unaffected by the growth of population a mile away. The primary school, St. Peter's CE School is expected to be closed when a new school is built at Shawbirch; a large proportion of its pupils have been from Admaston for many years. The small village shop, located in the old Boys' School, has had difficulty in surviving in the face of competition from Wellington supermarkets. But surprisingly few houses have been built in the village in recent years.

St. Peter's Church is, as it has been for perhaps a thousand years, the centre of the village; a Grade I listed building of many periods from Saxon onwards, a solid stone place standing on pre-Cambrian foundations. Unusually there is no village inn, a lack for which there seems no satisfactory explanation. The Hall, a large 17th and 18th century house is now the official home of the General in charge of Western Command.

Much of Wrockwardine belongs to the Orleton estate, which may have prevented it from being built up. It is a very mature village with families who have lived here for many generations, well used to resisting or coping with changes. In the meantime Wrockwardine has succeeded in preventing itself from being a lost village.

Wrockwardine Hall.

Bull's Head Inn.

Wrockwardine Wood Way.

66. WROCKWARDINE WOOD

Originally Wrockwardine Wood was a detached part of Wrockwardine parish, its parent village being four miles away. Domesday credits Wrockwardine as having 'woodland, one league long and ½ wide' which must be Wrockwardine Wood. However, as there was iron ore and coal very near the surface the mineral rights were more important by the 17th century than any income from timber or farming.

An iron ore mine was recorded in 1324, by which time the surface supply must have been exhausted. Regular mining, however, did not take place until the early 17th century. Joseph Banks describes a pit in Wrockwardine Wood where there were three layers of ironstone between coal beds. Uppermost were smooth iron nodules the size of potatoes, then a layer of stone and below that large lumps of iron weighing up to half a hundredweight set in blue clay or shale.

In 1731, Richard Hartshorne, the leading coal entrepreneur leased mining interests and sank new pits; soon there were mines at The Nab and The Moss. As Shropshire's coke-iron industry expanded the Coalbrookdale Company became the biggest customer and most of the iron was sent to Richard Reynolds' foundry at Ketley. Many of the mines were operated under a tenancy agreement by 'chartermasters' who employed labour and paid rent in the same way as tenant farmers.

From 1792 to 1841 there was an important glassworks in Wrockwardine Wood, using slag from the Donnington Wood furnaces, refractory bricks from Horsehay and basalt from Little Dawley. They made crown glass and dark green bottles for the French wine trade; also table ware, buttons, walking sticks and rolling pins. The closure was due to the Glass Duties Act of 1838. In 1856 the manager's house became the rectory and the works was converted to working class housing known as Glassworks Square.

In 1764 Richard Jones of Wellingon leased a clay mine in Brick Kiln Field. John Jones in 1783 made 209,000 bricks at the Nabb. The Lilleshall Company owned a brickworks there in 1850.

Holy Trinity Church was built in 1833 by Samuel and Thomas Smith of Madeley. It is in a plain Georgian style, with red brick and a square west tower.

Wrockwardine Wood House, part of which is now the Granville Hotel, is a large and interesting building, dated 1734, a hundred years older than the church. Across the road is a green and brown tiled Victorian pub, the Bull's Head, which is a listed building.'

The Cockshutt Piece — presumably once a place where wild birds were caught — has been preserved and is developing its own unique ecology.

Telford has done the village no favours by driving Wrockwardine Wood Way straight across the middle, cutting it in half. In spite of all this Wrockwardine Wood is still a recognisable community, even if a stranger would find it difficult to define its boundaries.

Holy Trinity Church.

MAP OF THE POPULATION OF TELFORD IN 1966

The distribution of population before the coming of the New Town. Each dot stands for 100 people and is approximately in the centre of those 100. The main concentration is in the north, at Wellington, Oakengates, Hadley and Donnington. In the centre is Dawley, with a large open space between there and Madeley and Ironbridge to the south. Compare this map with the latest from Telford Development Corporation and it is clear where the new buildings are. Before Telford the population was 69,200. Most of the spaces between the dots were farmland.

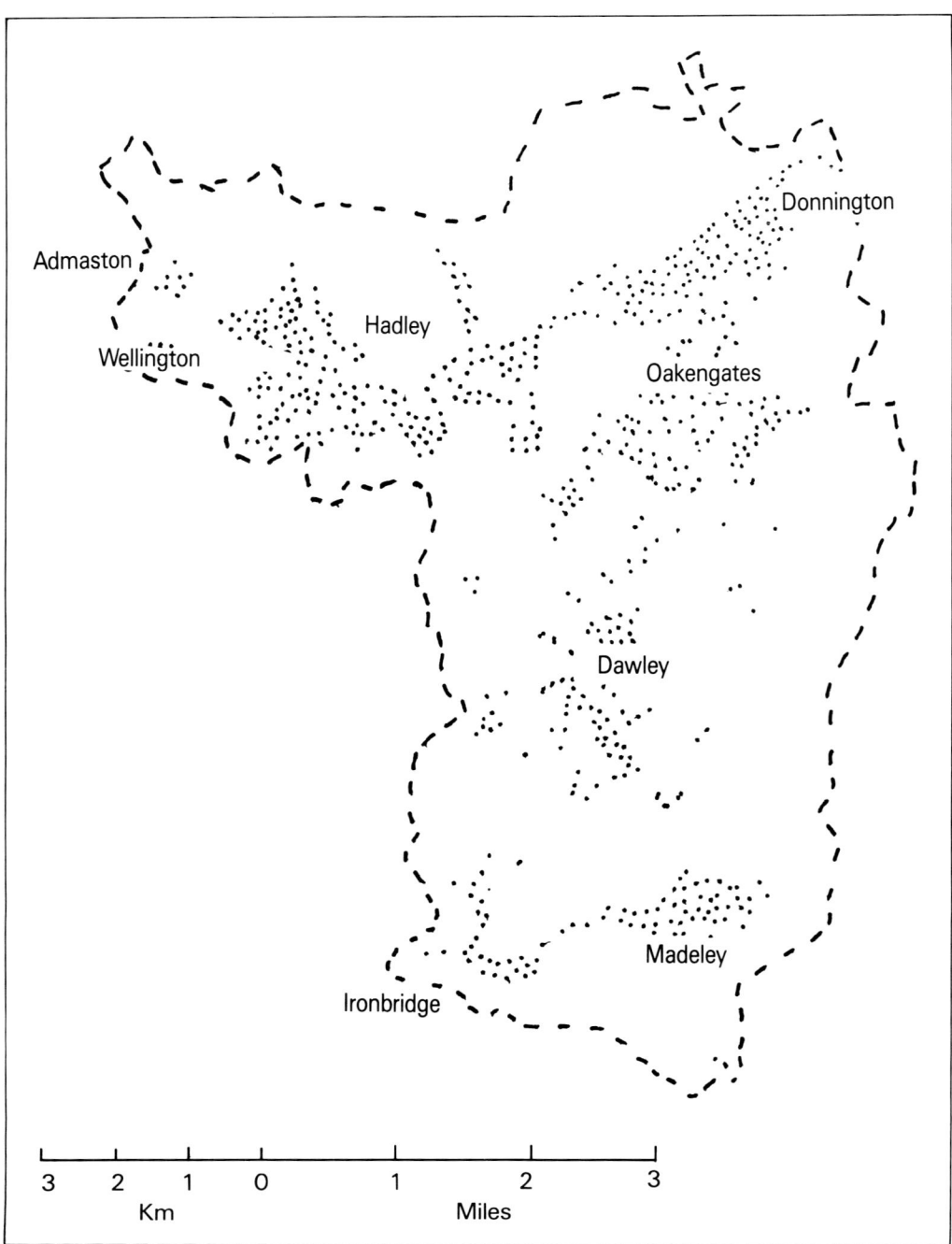

MAP OF BASIC GEOLOGY

This is not intended to be a comprehensive map of the geology of the area, which is far too complex to map in black and white or on this scale. It is mainly included to illustrate the commercially important rocks of the coalfield. For a more comprehensive map I recommend the Geological Survey's special 1:25,000 map of this very special district, though even that is not necessarily approximate.

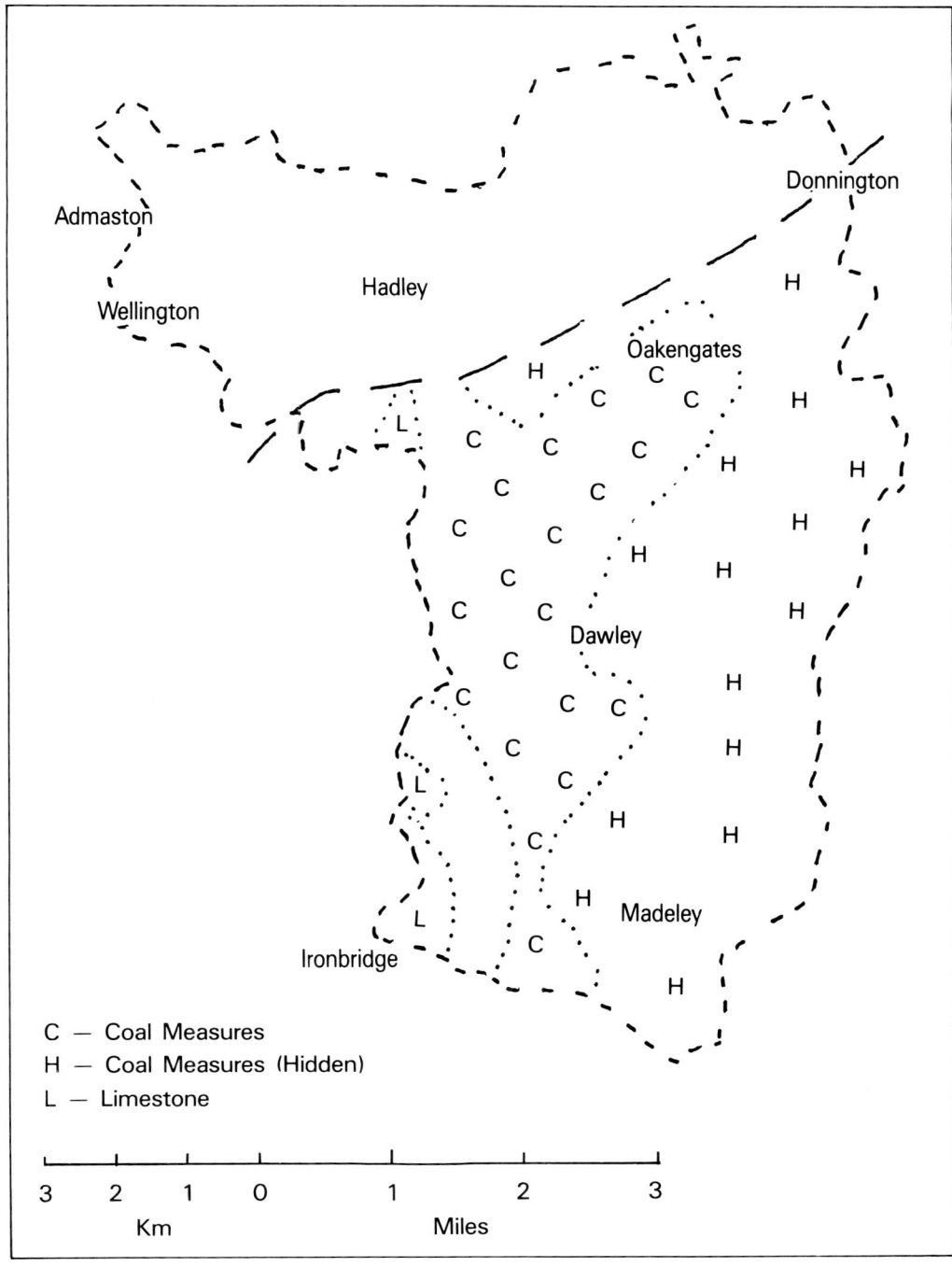

TELFORD IN 1808 — MAP BY ROBERT BAUGH

In 1808, 99 years after Abraham Darby's breakthrough with the use of coke in ironfounding, this was a very different place. There were canals and inclines but no railways. Some of the turnpike roads had not been completed and the iron bridge was still young. The strange line which wanders about is the boundary between the Hundred of South Bradford in the north and the Borough of Wenlock to the south. Wellington was the town; other important places were Wombridge, Priors Lee, Dawley Church, Great Dawley, Stirtchley and Madeley; Oaken Gates and Ironbridge were small hamlets. There are other historic maps to be seen at the local studies libraries in Wellington and Shrewsbury and like this one they are a fascinating study. Of course all maps are out of date by the time they are published but it is well worth preserving an old map for its historic interest.

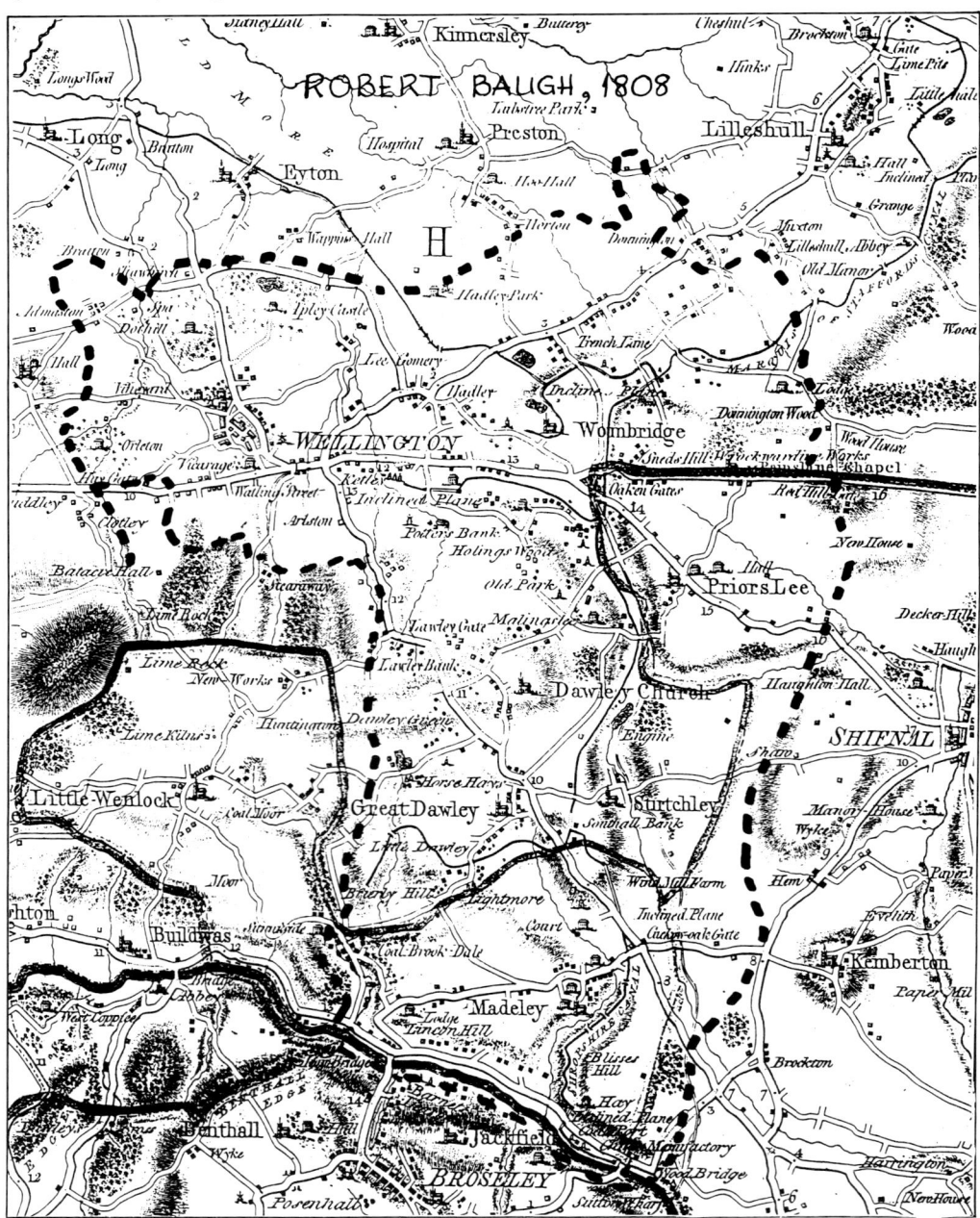

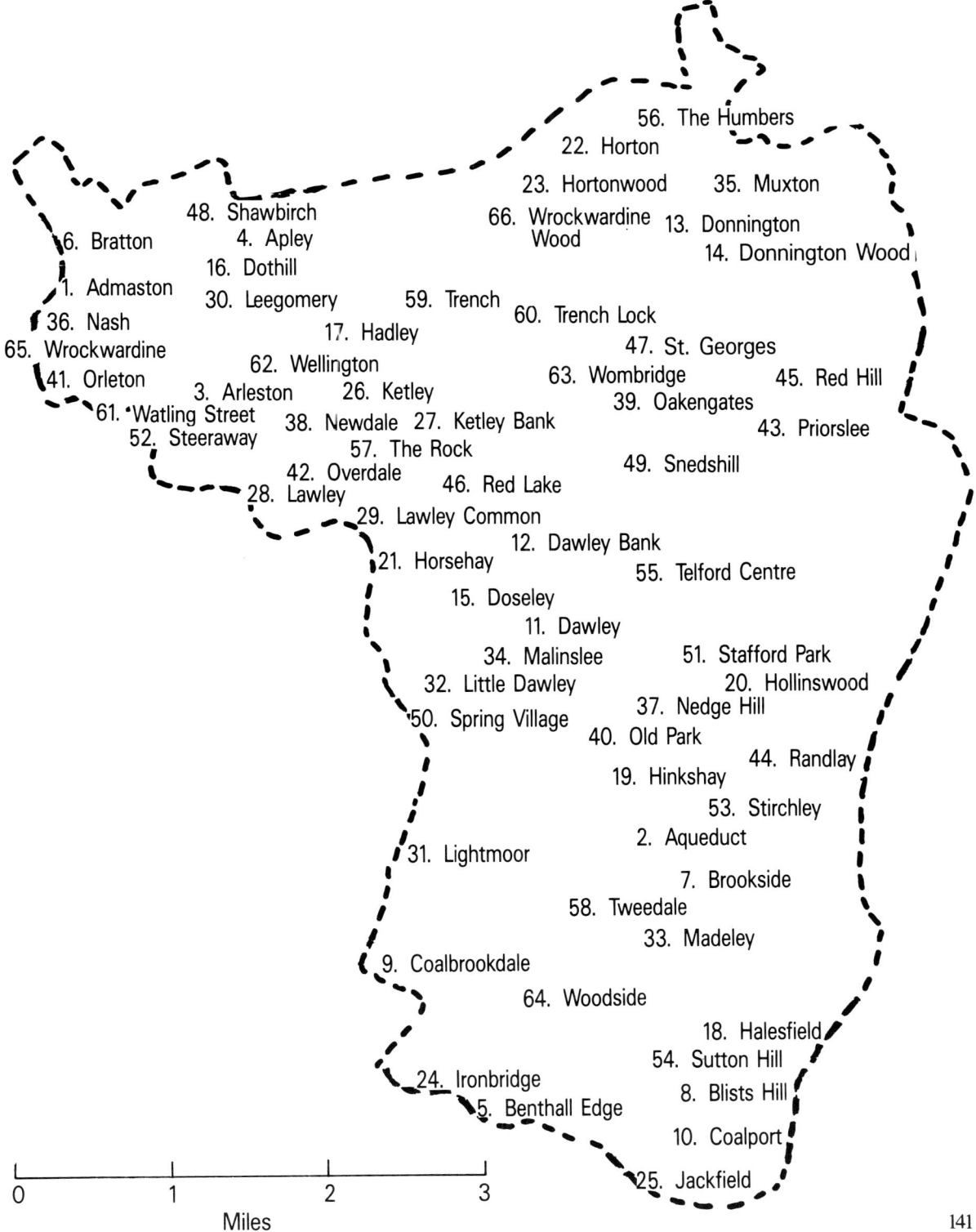

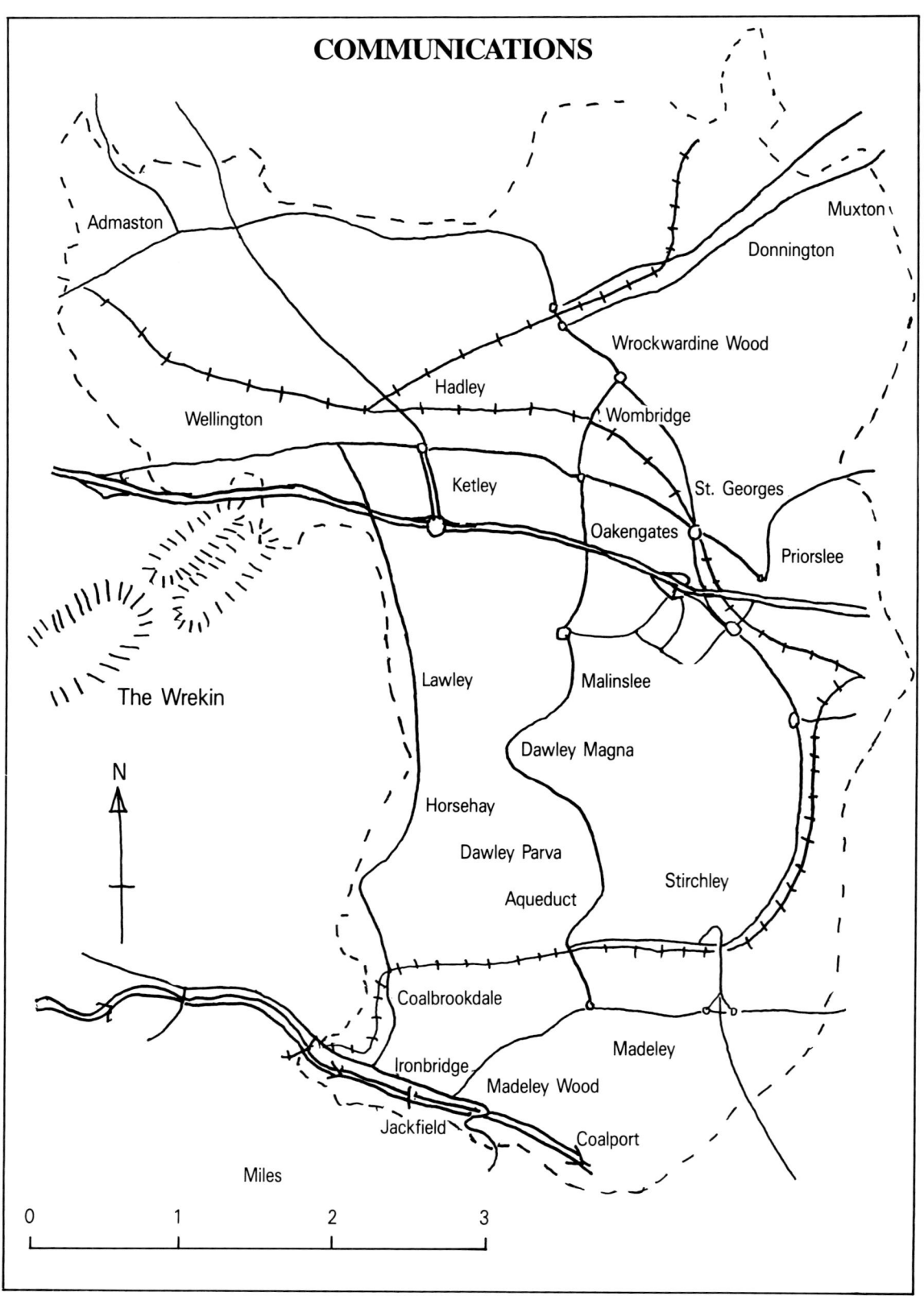

A BRIEF HISTORY OF THE AREA

Any trace of the first people to arrive here has been obliterated by the last Ice Age, which deposited clay, sand and gravel over the whole area except The Wrekin. We are sure they were here but there is no evidence to prove it.

There were certainly Neolithic and Bronze Age peoples before the Celts who rebuilt the hillfort on The Wrekin. This became our first real town, the headquarters of the Cornovii tribal lands extending as far as the Mersey. Two thousand years ago most of the mechanical tools and crafts we now use had been invented; there were markets, weaving, farming, fishing, metal workers, priests, teachers and entertainers. Our ancestors were intelligent people.

Then the Romans came, first as military conquerors. They built a planned New Town (there is nothing original in New Towns here!), called Viroconium, just the other side of The Wrekin from Telford. This was abandoned 1,500 years ago, perhaps because of the plague. There was then a small kingdom of the 'Wrekin Settlers' called Wreokensaete whose headquarters may have been Wrockwardine, with Wellington as the religious centre. The Mercians eventually took over, expanding as far as Wales and building Offa's Dyke.

By the time of the Normans the forest of The Wrekin, which had covered most of the land now in Telford, had already been cleared in many 'leys' — Hadley, Dawley, Madeley, Leegomery and so on, for farming. Wellington became the chief market and industries grew up in many villages. In the 18th century it became clear that the coal, iron and clay under the farmland were more valuable than the soil on the top. There was a great upsurge of mining and manufacturing on an increasingly large scale, making this area nationally and internationally important.

The boom, however, did not last. Communications, in spite of inventions such as inclined planes, were difficult and minerals ran out. Some industries flourished but many declined. By the 1960s although some places were relatively prosperous, there were pockets of decline. Central Government then decided to build a New Town here. There was little local consultation.

There have been several 'New Town' phases; at first Dawley, which began as an overspill for Birmingham, followed by a determined expansion which seemed rather brash. This was followed by a recession, but soon there was the M54 and new industry, a boom of 'executive' building and the buying of previously rented homes. Some communities disappeared, others struggled to survive; some were swamped by newcomers, others are newly created. But each of my sixty-six 'villages' is quite different from all the others. That is the charm of the place.

Now most of the infrastructure has been completed. The 'town centre' is looking more like the centre of a town, less like an American shopping mall. The trees are growing and Telford is beginning to mature. So much for history; we must now look to the future.

BIBLIOGRAPHY

Shropshire, Victoria County History, Vol. XI, Ed. G.C. Baugh — O.U.P.
A Shropshire Gazetteer, Michael Raven — M. Raven.
Shropshire, Domesday Book, Ed. F. & C. Thorn — Phillimore.
The Shropshire Village Book, — Shropshire Federation of WIs.
Yeoman & Colliers in Telford, Barrie Trinder — Phillimore.
The Most Extraordinary District in the World — Trinder.
A History of Shropshire, T. Auden — O.U.P.
Shropshire, The Geography of the County, W. W. Watts — Wilding.
Telford, Development Proposals, The John Madin Design Group.
The Shropshire Landscape, Trevor Rowley — Hodder & Stoughton.
The Lilleshall Company, Gale & Nicholas — Moorland Pub. Co.
Geology in Shropshire, P. Toghill — Swan Hill.
Shropshire County Handbooks 1960 & 1980, — S.C.C.
The Dawley Book, Ed. G. Peet & P. Garbett — Great Dawley P.C.
The Oakengates Book, — Oakengates Town Council.
The Hadley Book — Telford Community Arts.
Wellington Before Telford — Wellington Townswomen's Guild.
Memories of Old Wellington, Volumes I, II, & III — Civic Society.
Wellington in old Picture Postcards, G. Evans — European Library.
Wellington, a Portrait, — G. Evans — S. B. Publications.
Cassey's Directory of Shropshire, 1871.
Annual Land Statement, Wrekin Council, 1989.
Telford Local Plan, Wrekin Council, 1990.
Wellington U.D.C. 1894 — 1955.
The Wrekin Directory — 1962.
Wellington Rural District Guides, 1961 & 1966.
Methodism in Wellington, John Lenton, 1982.
The Old Dissent, 1700 — 1920, Rev. Dr. Harry Foreman.
Wellington U.D.C. Official Guide, 1949 & 1971.
Wellington, a Town with a Past — Laurens Otter.

Maps

1":1 mile Ordnance Survey, 1841 & 1961.
1:50,000 Ordnance Survey, Landranger 127, 1986.
1:25,000 Ordnance Survey, SJ 60 & 61. 1949 & 1981.
1:25,000 Ordnance Survey, Pathfinder 870 & 890, 1988.
6":1 mile Ordnance Survey, 1951.
25":1 mile Ordnance Survey 1936.
Telford Development Strategy, T.D.C., 1984.
Telford Local Plan, Wrekin Council, 1991.
Telford & Environs T.R. Bennett 1973.
Geology of Telford, 1:25,000, Inst. Geol. Sci.
1":1 mile land use maps 1932 & 1974 — Land Use Survey.
Telford Street Maps, 1980 & 1990 — T.D.C.
Tythe maps — various parishes, H.D.G.F. — S.C.C.
John Wood Map of Wellington, 1840.
C. & J. Greenwood, Shropshire, 1826-27.
Robert Baugh, Shropshire, 1808.
John Rocque, Shropshire, 1752.

S.B. Publications publish a wide range of local history books. For details write (enclosing S.A.E.) to: S.B. Publications, Unit 2, The Old Station Yard, Pipe Gate, Market Drayton, Shropshire TF9 4HY.